TOWARDS TONALIT

*This is the sixth publication in the series
"Collected Writings of the Orpheus Institute"
edited by Peter Dejans*

TOWARDS TONALITY

Aspects of Baroque
Music Theory

Thomas Christensen
Penelope Gouk
Gérard Geay
Susan McClary
Markus Jans
Joel Lester
Marc Vanscheeuwijck

COLLECTED WRITINGS OF THE

ORPHEUS
INSTITUTE

Leuven University Press
2007

CONTENTS

PREFACE / P. 07

— Thomas Christensen
Genres of Music Theory, 1650–1750 / P. 09

— Penelope Gouk
*Science and Music, or the Science of Music:
Some Little-known Examples of "Music Theory"
Between 1650 and 1750* / P. 41

— Gérard Geay
L'édition de la polyphonie française du 17e siècle / P. 71

— Susan McClary
Towards a History of Harmonic Tonality / P. 91

— Markus Jans
*Towards a History of the Origin and Development
of the Rule of the Octave* / P. 119

— Joel Lester
*Thoroughbass as a Path to Composition
in the Early Eighteenth Century* / P. 145

— Marc Vanscheeuwijck
*Giovanni Paolo Colonna and Petronio Franceschini:
Building Acoustics and Compositional Style
in Late Seventeenth-Century Bologna* / P. 171

PERSONALIA / P. 202

COLOPHON / P. 207

PREFACE

This is a collection of essays based on lectures presented at the *International Orpheus Academy for Music & Theory* on "Historical Theory, Performance, and Meaning in Baroque Music", April 14-18, 2004, at the Orpheus Institute, Ghent, Belgium.

The often complex connections and intersections between, e.g., modal and tonal idioms, contrapuntal and harmonic organisation, were considered from various perspectives as to the transition ("towards tonality") from the Renaissance to the Baroque era.

During lectures, lecture-performances, and group discussions, prominent guest musicians and scholars from a wide range of complementary fields testified to their personal understanding of the matter. We think their contributions will prove as illuminating for the reader as they were for the audience.

Please allow me to sincerely thank my co-editor Sylvester Beelaert for his critical acumen and accuracy.

Peter Dejans

GENRES OF MUSIC THEORY, 1650–1750

Thomas Christensen

To help make sense of any complex intellectual or historical discipline, scholars have usually found it necessary to divide the subject up into various classifications and parts that are related in some kind of rationalized network or hierarchy. Put more metaphorically, we create maps of disciplines by which to survey and understand the varied terrains we wish to navigate in our studies. Without some kind of order imposed upon either unwieldy empiricism or intellectual abstraction, our work as scholars and historians would be well-nigh impossible. Disciplinary categories and divisions are indispensable as cognitive heuristics.

Of course, divisions (or maps) of disciplines do not remain stable over time. This is particularly so in the case of music theory, whose domain and sub-categories have varied widely since the first extant theoretical writings from antiquity. What constitutes music theory over this 2000-year period—its primary subject matters and its attendant internal configurations—has changed dramatically. A difficulty for many students today, then, is to recognize and understand unfamiliar historical topographies. We can become so complacent as to what a subject such as music theory "looks like" from our own experiences and practice that it becomes quite jarring to observe radically differing conceptualizations. Topics that we might presume belong inherently to music theory may not be found in older writings, while conversely, other topics that we would not associate at all with the discipline of theory are in fact featured prominently. For that matter, it may not even be clear what literature we ought to look at as constituting music theory.[1]

---

1. A thoughtful meditation on the knotty epistemological and historiographical problems of mapping music theory is found in Lee Blasius, "Mapping the Terrain", in: Thomas Christensen (ed.), *The Cambridge History of Western Music Theory*, Cambridge 2002, pp. 27–45.

There is perhaps no historical period in which we can find more dramatic juxtapositions of "older" and "newer" conceptions of music theory than the period 1650–1750. Framed by works such as Athanasius Kircher's *Mursurgia Universalis* (1650) and René Descartes's *Compendium Musicae* (published in 1650, although first penned around 1618) on the one end, and Jean-Philippe Rameau's *Démonstration du principe de l'harmonie* (1750) and Jean-Jacques Rousseau's first musical articles for the great *Encyclopédie* (1751) on the other, we traverse a bewildering number of musical writings that seem to elude coherent synthesis. Admittedly, any centenary demarcation of a historical period is an artificial one. Still, it is hard to recognize even minimal intellectual conformity in the music-theoretical writings of a time span that includes such diverse figures as Kircher, Descartes, Rameau and Rousseau, not to mention Roger North, Andreas Werckmeister, Joseph Sauveur, Lorenzo Penna, Johann Mattheson, and Leonhard Euler (to offer only a random selection of names). Even if we agree that the music composed between 1650 and 1750 evinces a bit more holism (and this is itself subject to strong challenge, given that music historians have by and large been moving away from the older historical model of a High Baroque Period "terminating" at mid-century with the deaths of Bach and Handel), there is certainly no reason to presume that music theory must necessarily follow suit.

The problem, however, may be not so much that of the time we are considering than that of the subject of music theory itself, which (as we have already noted) has always been historically diverse in its contents and methods. In order to make sense of the richness and complexity of music-theoretical thought between 1650 and 1750 — or from any period, for that matter — we need to establish some criteria by which to decide what writings in fact constitute "music theory". We won't necessarily find help by simply reading the title pages of books, for few authors on musical matters at the time would have referred to their writings as "theoretical", let alone called themselves "theorists". What we need to do is agree upon a broad definition of music theory that is flexible enough to accommodate many of the writings of this period that would otherwise elude classification, while at the same time having enough internal coherence so as to provide a meaningful basis of inclusion.² In short, we need a good map of the music-theoretical terrain of the early modern period.

As a point of departure, I have found it useful to invoke a tripartite classification of music theory first suggested as far as I am aware by Carl Dahlhaus. In his brilliant monograph on the history of eighteenth- and nineteenth-century music theory, Dahlhaus has identified three broad traditions into which Western music theory may be divided: speculative, regulative, and analytic.³ Simply put, speculative theory concerns the "ontological contemplation" of musical essences and materials, their basis in number and acoustics. (This science often went by the name of "harmonics" in antiquity.) Historically speaking, speculative harmonics was the oldest and most authentic sense in which music theory was understood by musicians through the seventeenth century. "Regulative" theory, according to Dahlhaus, constitutes the broad range of "practical" and "poetical" writings that instructed students on the rudiments and syntactic rules of music, encompassing such topics as pitch notation, mode, rhythm, meter, counterpoint, harmony, and form. (Today, such pedagogical writings are often considered to be the epitome of music theory, although historically such writings were usually classified as "musica practica" or "musica poetica" rather than "musica theorica".) Finally, a third, more critical tradition arose in the late eighteenth and early nineteenth centuries (although there were a few notable precedents already in the early seventeenth century) that can be roughly

---

2. I have pondered in greater detail some of the hermeneutic problems alluded to in this paragraph of reifying and historicizing a given period of music theory in an older article of mine, "Music Theory and its Histories", in: David Bernstein (Ed.), *Music Theory and the Exploration of the Past*, Chicago 1993, pp. 23–51. Also of relevance to this question is the recent essay of Dörte Schmidt, "Handlungsräume. Von der 'Universal-Geschichte' zu einer 'Kulturgeschichte' der Musiktheorie", in: Dörte Schmidt (ed.), *Musiktheoretisches Denken und kultureller Kontext*, Schliengen 2005, pp. 9–17.
3. Carl Dahlhaus, *Die Musiktheorie im 18. und 19. Jahrhundert: I, Grundzüge einer Systematik*, Darmstadt 1984. See especially pp. 9–13. Also see Dahlhaus's historiographical essay, "Was heißt 'Geschichte der Musiktheorie'?", in: Frieder Zaminer (ed.), *Ideen zu einer Geschichte der Musiktheorie. Einleitung in das Gesamtwerk. Geschichte der Musiktheorie vol. 1*, Darmstadt 1985, p. 39.

grouped within the locution of "music analysis". Here the concern is with the intensive study and contemplation of musical masterworks as models for compositional study and aesthetic appreciation.

I find it helpful to think of these traditions as "genres" of theory, as odd as they may sound to us as a locution. (Dahlhaus himself, it should be noted, chooses to call these "paradigms" of music theory after the historian of science, Thomas Kuhn.) Much like a musical genre, each of these theoretical paradigms has certain fundamental characteristics unique to itself that nonetheless are manifest in multiple ways in practice. At the same time, as genres, each belongs to a common "family" of critical and pedagogical writings that we can group heuristically as "music theory". Thinking of music theory in terms of genre has helped me to make some sense of the bewildering varieties of musical writings we find in the history of music theory—and particularly from the late seventeenth and early eighteenth centuries.[4]

In the following essay, I propose to consider how the three genres of music theory outlined by Dahlhaus look in the period 1650–1750. We will see that each of the genres of theory changed in fundamental ways over the course of this time. Indeed, in many ways, the modern institutional character and configuration of music theory is one that first came into view during this period. Yet we will also see how less familiar conceptions of music theory that were legacies of early thought and practice continued to play out in the seventeenth and eighteenth centuries. I should emphasize that the following essay should by no means be mistaken for a comprehensive survey of Baroque music theory. That is clearly impossible within its limited scope. But what I do hope to do is sketch out with selected examples some of the major themes of Baroque music theory—a general map, if you will, of the chang-

---

4. Indeed, I have ended up organizing my own history of theory project directly around this tripartite division, although I have modified his model in significant ways (cited in footnote 1). In the Introduction to this history, I have expounded at some length many of the points I am making in the present article (pp. 1–23).

ing topographies of the music-intellectual landscape. By considering the historical roots and epistemological tensions of music theory during this seminal time frame, we will better understand how those same tensions continue to reverberate today.

1

Let me begin with the branch of speculative theory discussed by Dahlhaus. As I have already indicated, this is unquestionably the oldest and in many ways most authentic genre of music theory. Indeed, it was the only sense in which *musica theorica* was understood by most musicians well into the eighteenth century. What was the nature of *musica theorica*? Here we must return for a moment to ancient Greece, where some of the very first writings on music were penned. It was Greek philosophers, too, who articulated the epistemological framework within which *theoria* was understood.

Let us begin by reminding ourselves of the etymology of the term *theoria*. It comes from the Greek word to contemplate, observe, or behold: *theoreo*. A *theoros* was a spectator at a game. *Theoria* as an activity leads to a kind of knowledge—*epistēmē*—that Aristotle contrasted with practical knowledge and skills—*technē*.

If there was no recognized profession of music theorist in Ancient Greece, there was an occupation we can inelegantly translate as the "theoretical contemplator of musical elements". But this occupation went under a simpler title: a musician. If you were a musician in Ancient Greece—a *mousikos*—it meant you understood the nature and essence of music's material. In a tenacious Platonic tradition (whose roots are traceable back to the Pythagoreans), this nature and essence of music consisted of number and ratio. A true musician understood the mathematical basis of musical material. It did not mean that one knew how to write, sing, or play music. Indeed, most probably a *mousikos* could have done none of these things.

I can make this non-intuitive distinction clearer, perhaps, by looking at the famous tripartite organization of music laid down in the sixth century by that greatest synthesizer and transmitter of

Greek musical thought, Boethius. (See Ex. 1.) Now it may seem odd that I turn to a writer active in the sixth century of the Christian era as a representative of ancient classical music theory articulated a full millennium earlier. Yet in many ways, there was no more faithful representative of the Platonic ideal of musical *theoria* than Boethius.

Example 1. Boethius, De institutione musica *(6th Century AD)*

1. Musica Mundana	2. Musica Humana	3. Musica Instrumentalis
a. Celestial Objects	a. Animal Spirits	a. Tension (string)
b. The Four Elements	b. Body	b. Spirit (wind)
c. Temporal (seasons)	c. Temperament	c. Percussion
("Musicus")	("Poet")	("Executor")

As any student of music history well knows, Boethius argued that there were three basic kinds of music: *mundana, humana,* and *instrumentalis*— the harmony of the spheres, of the human body, and finally of instrumental music.[5] Implicated within the Platonic cosmology, these musics represented three distinct species of *harmonia* or consonance, each one itself divisible into three sub-categories. And need I emphasize that of the three kinds of music, *musica instrumentalis* was the one holding the least interest or ethical value to Boethius, it being the most corrupted, profane form of harmonia, coming as it does from the hands of man, and the only one perceptible by the mortal ear.

Still, as a science concerned with numerical relations and harmonia, Boethius was able to incorporate music into the great Quadrivium of mathematical sciences, along with arithmetic, geometry, and astronomy. As Boethius explained it (although drawing heavily upon earlier Neoplatonic traditions), arithmetic was the science of numbers without mobility and without extension; geometry was the science of numbers without mobility, but

---

5. See Boethius, *Fundamentals of Music*, trans. Calvin M. Bower, New Haven 1989, Book 1, ch. 2.

with extension; astronomy, however, dealt with magnitudes with both mobility and extension, while music was the science of magnitudes with mobility but lacking extension.

Now Boethius mapped onto his division of three kinds of musical harmonia the three professions of music that corresponded to their ontological value: one who judges music, one who writes music, and one who plays a musical instrument. Let me take these in reverse order. The instrumentalist, the executor, Boethius tells us, is like a servant—one totally dedicated to the performance of his instrument and bearing nothing of reason or spirit, "being wholly destitute of speculation" as he put it. The composer, or inventor of songs, however, can be compared to the poet. He is "borne to song not so much by speculation and reason as by a certain natural instinct." And it is for this reason that Boethius pairs the composer with *musica humana*—like the poet, the composer relies on the animal spirits and passions of the body for inspiration, the exhaling of *spiritus* through his breath and song. Finally, there is the person who judges music by reason and speculation, understanding the mathematical nature and cause of harmonia in all its forms. For Boethius—as for Plato—this was the real musician, indeed, the only one who properly deserves the name:

> And seeing that the whole is founded in reason and speculation, this class is rightly reckoned as musical, and that man as a musician who possesses the faculty of judging, according to speculation or reason, appropriate and suitable to music, of modes and rhythms and of the classes of melodies and their mixtures…

A musician, then, was one who understood the ontological nature of music, which is to say, its numerical essence. The ability to perform or compose was secondary. Aristotle would have contrasted these kinds of knowledge as knowing an object's final cause, its formal and material cause, and its efficient cause. The instrumentalist knows only the efficient cause of music—the mechanical production of sounds, like a worker who builds a house. The composer, however, knows the material and formal causes of music, what a composition is made of and how it is put together, much as does the designer or architect of the house. But only the true musician understands music's final cause: its ultimate nature, purpose and function—the reason, we might say, why the house was built in the first place.

It is perhaps odd to be citing Aristotle here in support of Boethius's hyper-Platonic metaphysics. But Aristotle would have had no disagreement in strongly demarcating practical from theoretical elements of music, just as he would distinguish poetics from practice and theory. His concern would lie with the kinds of *theoria* to be invoked—what is the best method for attaining true knowledge and understanding of music. He certainly never would have questioned the superiority of understanding the formal and final cause of an object over its efficient or material causes.

To be sure, Aristotle would have argued that to gain access to the essence of an object, one needs to go through perceptual appearance—its *phainomenon*. We need only recall briefly the views of that arch-empiricist and student of Aristotle, Aristoxenus of Tarentum. With characteristic bluster and arrogance, Aristoxenus lambasted the followers of Plato who would judge music on criteria of number and form. For Aristoxenus, the musician must use empirical evidence of the ear. But by this, he does not mean going into the Elysian Fields and listening to performers of the aulos, or rhapsodes reciting Homer to the accompaniment of a kithara. As far as their musical worth was concerned, Aristoxenus could be just as supercilious as any Platonist. Rather, Aristoxenus meant a kind of internal, almost phenomenological conceptualization of musical material. For this purpose, he insisted upon beginning with the voice-conceiving and defining intervals and genera by listening to the voice inflecting them rather than abstractly plotting interval ratios.

In all of the ancient writings I have drawn from so far, it is worth emphasizing how disassociated concerns of practical music were for these classical music theorists. To be sure, we can find discussions of *tonoi* and the varieties of *genera* and *systemata* by Aristoxenus. But these can hardly be called practical constructs. They represented a mixture of idealized historical reconstructions and abstracted systematization of tonal materials—not things that ever had any real musical meaning to singers or instrumentalists. And by the time we come to authorities like Aristides Quintilianus writing some 500 years after Aristoxenus, which is to say, about the second century of the modern era — the distance between theory and practice was even greater.

Still, this did not stop Aristides from suggesting his own comprehensive mapping of music that gave prominent room to musical practice, shown in Ex. 2.[6]

Example 2.: Aristides Quintilianus, De Musica *(2nd Century AD)*

1. *Theoretikon*   2. *Praktikon*

A. Natural (*physikon*)   A. Creative (*chrestikon*)
   1. Arithmetical   1. Melo-poetic
   2. Natural   2. Temporal
                                      3. Poetic

B. Artificial (*technikon*)   B. Executive (*exangeltikon*)
   1. Harmonic   1. Instrumental
   2. Rhythmic   2. Vocal
   3. Metric   3. Dramatic

As we see, Aristides recognized two parts of practical music — composition and performance — the creative and executive. Neither of them, of course, could be considered relevant to true musicians. Aristides was too much of a Platonist for such charity. Observe, also, that Aristides distinguishes two parts to the theoretical category: natural and artificial. By natural elements of music, he distinguishes numerical and acoustical ways of defining music — while under artificial music (*technikon*) he means the primary parameters of *musica instrumentalis* — to bring us back (or more accurately, forward) to Boethius. Remember, too, this is

---

6. Aristides Quintilianus, *On Music in Three Books*, trans. Thomas J. Mathiesen, New Haven 1983. While Aristides never himself synthesized his divisions of music into the neat graph shown in Ex. 1, I was inspired by Claude Palisca's adaptation of Aristides's taxonomy as a basis for his important entry "Theory" in the *New Grove Dictionary of Music and Musicians*, London 1980.

not harmony, rhythm or meter in any sense that would be useful to those sympathetic to the second column of practical music. Rather, these are the kinds of potential relationships latent in sounding music.

Observe, finally, while both taxonomies maintain the opposition between theory and practice, each does so in very different styles. Boethius's opposition lies on a continuum. It depicts a hierarchy or chain of being with Platonic overtones, its presentation accordingly emphasizes continuity and contiguity. For Aristides, however, this opposition is dialectical. Following the model of Aristotelian logic, his categories are oppositional; his presentation accordingly is tabular and schematic.

It is possible, then, to form a composite conceptual definition of *musica theorica* as predominantly speculative in the ancient world based on the writings of Aristoxenus, Aristides, Nicomachus, not to mention many of the others whose writings have come down to us in various degrees of corruption. For all their differences in style and philosophy, their unified concern was the ontology of music — its material, nature, and meaning — but not its practice, not as it was composed, played, and heard by anyone of their day — or any day, really.

The subsequent development of music theory in the Latinized west — the move in other words, from Greek to Latin *theoria* — may be generally characterized as a process of growing tension between speculative and practical traditions — the concerns, pedagogical needs and activities of singers increasingly tugging at those of the theorists. Of course in one sense it is an oxymoron to speak of "practical theory". Any rapprochement of theory and practice is conceptually subversive, as it threatens the very epistemological grounding upon which Greek *theoria* had been based. In other words, the strong demarcation between the realms of theory and practice was the condition upon which theory as a discipline could exist.

This is why, at least on the surface, various kinds of distinctions continued to be maintained between theory and practice in the medieval period. We find, for instance, Guido famously distinguishing *cantor* and *musicus*. The *musicus* — the music theorist — is one who understands the nature of music, and stands in contrast to the poor ignorant singer—the *cantor*—who Guido reminds us, "is the most foolish of men".[7]

But I need not also remind you that Guido did indeed concern himself with singers and their practical needs. His *Micrologus*, after all, is a handbook for singers, and it is there that Guido introduced his revolutionary notational system and the equally famous solfège mnemonic for navigating the tonal space of the hexachord. (By the way, Guido nowhere discusses the use of the hand to teach hexachordal mutations, despite that his name became attached to this method in the writings of subsequent theorists.) Indeed, by all accounts, with the Carolingian Renaissance, *musica theorica* in its orthodox, Boethian forms of cosmological harmonia and monochord divisions receded strongly in favor of *musica practica* or—as it was usually called thanks to the influential terminology adopted from the Arabic writer, Al-Farabi—*musica activa*. The concerns of the practicing singer became pressing, and music theory now assumed a regulative role that it has in large part retained to this day.

This pedagogical tradition of music theory (and here I am using "music theory" in a non-historical sense) is first evident in the West in several Carolingian manuscripts dating from the ninth and tenth centuries that sought to answer the Church's growing needs to systematize, codify, and notate a growing liturgical chant practice. This entailed solving several problems that have served as an agenda of music-theoretical topics ever since: clarifying a tonal space in which this music was sung, finding a vocabulary for analyzing the structure of a chant, a way of classifying the different species (or "modes") of chant represented, and finally, an efficient notation for setting down these chants so that they could be practiced and disseminated. Later on, other notational problems arose to which these theorists turned their attention, including the need to conceptualize a temporal space within which the rhythmic proportions and metrical subdivisions of music could be notated.

---

7. Quoted in Calvin Bower, "The Transmission of Ancient Music Theory into the Middle Ages", in: *The Cambridge History of Western Music Theory*, p. 163.

In many ways, the concern of theorists since the eleventh century have not changed radically. The diatonic gamut of Guido was expanded over the following centuries to include chromatic and enharmonic spaces. The structural vocabulary to analyze the components of a chant were expanded to include the more complex elements of counterpoint and harmony. Problems of mode classification gave way to problems of the major/minor key system, and ultimately questions over the nature of tonality itself. The parsing of chant melodies into discrete functional elements not only can be seen as a nascent form of music analysis, but as a precursor to later theoretical investigations of form.

We thus find a seismic shift in the concerns of the *musicus* towards a more practical bent. To be sure, *musica speculativa* in the tradition of ancient harmonics continued to be cultivated by some scholars; but its Platonic components were greatly diminished in the Universities thanks to the triumph of Aristotle's teaching in the Middle Ages via his Arabic transmitters. The cosmological and ethical elements of *musica mundana* and *humana* largely went into hibernation not to be revived in any major way until the re-emergence of Platonism in the late fifteenth century. Then, humanist scholars such as Franchino Gaffurio wrote once again on topics of *musica speculativa*, often drawing heavily upon the writings of Greek authors who were increasingly being translated and published. (It was Gaffurio, incidentally, who was the first to actually entitle one of his treatises as music theory: the *Theorica Musice* of 1492.) The concerns of Gaffurio were with ancient Quadrivial problems of musical sound, proportions, and tuning—in other words the classical agenda of ancient harmonics—as well as the more speculative matters of *musica mundana* and *humana*. And as a good humanist, Gaffurio was explicit about the virtues of *theoria* providing the most exalted knowledge of music. Troping from both Boethius and Aristotle, he writes:

> Accordingly, this discipline [that is, music], because it is a natural science, prefers the speculative or theoretical intellect as nobler and wiser than the practical... The speculative musician, then, is he who, led by reasoning, has acquired the science of singing not by the drudgery of practice but by the power of speculation ... Of this class

we call [him] a knowledgeable geometrician who has learned this science and retains it. Both [the speculative and the practical intellects] potentially know, but not in the same sense, for the former [does so] a little dimly and very tenuously only because he is teachable and capable of learning, whereas the other goes beyond, because he can contemplate an action and comment on it if not prevented by an external cause.[8]

Given his obvious epistemological bias, then, it may seem surprising to us that Gaffurio also took it upon himself to publish four years later a *Practica Musice* (1496) that dealt with contemporaneous problems of mode, mensuration, and counterpoint. In that work, Gaffurio seemed to have softened his stance some, granting a good deal more value to the poor *cantor* of musical practice:

> It is true that ... sounds are assembled in vain by theory and science unless they are expressed in practice. Hence one must become thoroughly conversant with the highness, lowness, and the combinations of these sounds not only through one's mind and reason but also through the habit of listening to and articulating them.[9]

Ultimately, one supposes, Gaffurio saw theory and practice as complementary, each necessary to the other, although still placing practice in an ontologically subordinate role to theory. But he also clearly knew where his bread was coming from. There was a good deal more of a market for a useable text of *musica practica* than for one of abstract theory. And in any case, if it was the role of theory to help guide and correct practice, then who else is in a better position to write such a practical treatise than the *musicus* who is versed in learned theory? Thus, after Gaffurio, it was commonplace to find treatises of *musica theorica* and *musica practica* paired together. Zarlino's *Le Istitutioni harmoniche* (1558) is only one of the most famous examples, its first two books constituting the

---

8. Franchino Gaffurio, *The Theory of Music*, trans. by Walter Kurt Kreyszig, New Haven 1993, pp. 41–42.
9. Irwin Young (ed. & trans.), *The Practica Musicae of Franchinus Gafurius*, Madison 1969, p. 12.

traditional agenda of speculative theory, and its last two books practical considerations of counterpoint and mode.[10]

2

By the beginning of the seventeenth century, then, we find two venerable traditions of musical thought standing in dialectical juxtaposition: *theorica* and *practica*.[11] Virtually all writers on musical topics acknowledged these two fundamental categories, sometimes with extended discussions concerning the epistemological value of each.[12] Still, the vast majority of musical literature we find published during the seventeenth century was of a practical nature. After all, it was the growing class of amateur musicians wishing to learn the rudiments of reading, playing, and composing music who provided a demand for such literature. Thus we

---

10. Not that Zarlino's first two books were devoid of practical considerations. Not only did Zarlino include various species of temperaments in Book II that were obviously driven by performance questions, he also famously introduced his *senario* to accommodate and legitimize the imperfect consonances that were then in common practice.
11. One might argue that another category should be introduced here: that of *musica poetica*. For German theorists of the seventeenth century, *musica poetica* constituted an important third category of musical study, it being concerned with the compositional process and work (*opus*) of music. As Nicolaus Listenius wrote in his *Rudimenta musicae planae* of 1537 (in which the term *musica poetica* was first used), "Poetica is that which strives neither for knowledge of things nor for mere practice, but leaves behind some work after the labor" (Poetica, quae neque rei cognitione, neque solo exercitio contenta, sed aliquid post laborem relinquit operis). (Wittenberg 1537, fol. A4v.) Joachim Burmeister's *Musica poetica* of 1600 is one of the classical exemplars of this genre, as well as works of Heinrich Faber, Gallus Dressler, and Sethus Calvisius. But as we will see, most "compositional theory" was integrated within works of *musica practica*, which held out composition as the end goal of their instructions, whether it was in the study of counterpoint or harmony, or in performance practice of instrumental diminution, vocal embellishment, or thoroughbass. (This is why Walther, in his *Lexikon* of 1732 ended up subsuming *musica poetica* within *musica practica*.) In any event, Heinz von Loesch has recently argued that any equation of the seventeenth-century German notion of the musical artwork with the nineteenth-century Romantic work-concept is based on a fundamental misunderstanding of Reformation aesthetic values. See his *Der Werkbegriff in der protestantischen Musiktheorie des 16. und 17. Jahrhunderts: Ein Mißverständnis*, Hildesheim 2001.
12. Mersenne in his *Questions harmoniques* of 1634 pondered whether "theory was to be preferred to practice" or vice versa. (Typically for Mersenne, he equivocated on the answer, although he did seem ultimately to come down in favor of theory.)

find, to take one typical example, a work such as Thomas Morley's *A Plaine and Easie Introduction to Practicall Musicke* (first published in 1597, but reissued as late as 1771), which was written for those who are "altogether unlearned or then have not so far proceeded in learning as to understand the reason of a definition."[13] The agenda of Morley's comprehensive treatise offered a typical (if unusually detailed) survey of topics in *musica practica*: the rudiments of pitch and rhythm ("Teaching to Sing"), counterpoint ("Treating of Descant"), and harmony ("Treating of Composing or Setting of Songs"). Dozens of other such works were published throughout Europe during the seventeenth century hoping to meet the increasing demand of amateur musicians for practical introductions to the skills of music.

Of course we continue to find more learned, speculative treatises of music theory published through the seventeenth and eighteenth centuries, if in vastly smaller numbers. The filiation of many of these early-modern treatises of theory to their counterparts in antiquity and the Middle Ages is clear not simply from their title pages (in which most explicitly contain references to "theory") but in their canonist agenda. Almost without exception, a "music theory" treatise in the seventeenth or eighteenth century was concerned with traditional problems of interval calculation and tuning.[14] The one major difference, however, was the kinds of

---

13. Thomas Morley, *A Plaine and Easie Introduction to Practicall Music*, London 1597; modern edition by Alec R. Harman, New York 1973, p. 100. Still, this did not prevent Morley from appending to his treatise some lengthy "annotations" in which more speculative and learned matters were raised for the benefit of those with "better skill in letters".

14. A representative sampling of such theory titles is suggestive: Otto Gibel, *Introductio musicae theoreticae didacticae... cum primis vero mathematica*, Bremen 1660; Thomas Salmon, *The Theory of Musick Reduced to Arithmetical and Geometric Proportions*, London 1705; Leonhard Euler, *Tentamen novae theoriae musicae*, St. Petersburg 1739; Friedrich Wilhelm Marpurg, *Anfangsgründe der theoretischen Musik*, Leipzig 1757; Giovanni Battista Martini, *Compendio della theoria de' numeri per uso del musico*, Bologna 1769. Jean-Philippe Rameau's *Nouveau système de musique théorique et pratique* of 1726 is also in the tradition, it being "new" only in the sense that it substituted an acoustical principle—the *corps sonore*—as the origin of musical proportions for the canonical one in string divisions (as was proposed in his *Traité de l'harmonie* four years earlier).

tunings being discussed, or more accurately, the kinds of temperaments. Using an array of new mathematical tools that were developed in the seventeenth century—above all that of logarithms—theorists were now able to calculate and test a dizzying number of new temperaments. If many of these temperaments were ultimately speculative "paper temperaments", we nonetheless see how practical considerations of musical performance were impinging upon the domain of speculative theory.[15]

But we cannot limit our consideration of speculative theory texts only to those that dealt with issues of temperament. With the revolutionary upheaval in scientific thought of the seventeenth century, music theory was also reinvigorated with new tools of inquiry and new domains of analysis. Particularly in the nascent field of acoustics and rational mechanics, scientists like Galileo Galilei, Marin Mersenne, Isaac Beeckman, and Isaac Newton can be said to have carried on the tradition of ancient harmonics with studies of the nature of sound propagation, the behavior of vibrating strings, and the acoustical basis of consonance and dissonance. The numerical criteria by which consonance had traditionally been determined and evaluated was slowly replaced in the seventeenth century with a mechanistic model in which consonance was analyzed and categorized according to frequency coincidence.[16] The culmination of this work is surely found in the writings of the French scientist Joseph Sauveur, who was the first to designate the scientific study of sound as "acoustique". In a series of important publications that appeared in the records of the *Académie Royale des Sciences* beginning in 1700, Sauveur was one of the first to subject musical sound to rigorous empirical analysis

---

15. An interesting exception to this was Descartes's *Compendium Musicae*. It is a traditional monograph in the canonist tradition dividing the monochord in order to generate the basic whole-number consonances of tonal practice. But if Descartes's topic was not original, his epistemological underpinnings in the treatise were. Beginning with a sensory phenomenology of sound from which he was able to deduce in methodical order the intervals of musical practice, the *Compendium* can be viewed as a test-case for the philosopher's evolving rationalist philosophy.

16. A story comprehensively treated in H. F. Cohen, *Quantifying Music: The Science of Music at the First Stage of the Scientific Revolution, 1580–1650*, Dordrecht 1984.

and experimental method. Among the musical topics he treated were the measurement and determination of fixed pitch, a highly-detailed logarithmic calculation of musical temperament, the mechanics of the vibrating string, and the overtone series.[17]

To be sure, other, more esoteric types of speculative theory were penned in the seventeenth century. Most conspicuous, perhaps, are those writings of the English Rosicrucian Robert Fludd and the German Jesuit, Athanasius Kircher (mentioned at the beginning of this essay), both of whom mixed into their musical writings speculations of cosmic harmony, gnostic lore, hermetic magic, alchemy, and Galenic medicine. Likewise, much of Kepler's writings on music are rooted in an older Quadrivial tradition in which music and cosmology were intimately entwined.[18] None of this should be surprising, since for a number of intellectual *virtuosi* of the seventeenth century, the boundary between "science" and "natural magic" was a porous one. As historians of science have pointed out, many of the problems and methods of early modern science are intimately enmeshed with natural magic, alchemy, and other occult sciences.[19] But even for those writers who eschewed natural magic or hermetic philosophy, the boundaries of music theory could be slippery.

The late seventeenth-century German theorist Andreas Werckmeister believed the new mechanistic sciences offered a wondrous, natural basis for understanding and explaining musical phenomena. At the same time, though, Werckmeister could not resist indulging in a great deal of numerical speculations and theological musings in his music theory. Hence, even a seemingly

---

17. See Joseph Sauveur, *Collected Writings on Musical Acoustics (Paris 1700–13)*, ed. Rudolf Rasch, Utrecht 1984. It was in fact Sauveur's demonstration of the harmonic partials in a periodically-vibrating body that was to be so influential to Rameau's own musical theories.
18. For Kepler's writings on music theory, see Bruce Stephenson, *The Music of the Heavens: Kepler's Harmonic Astronomy*, Princeton 1984.
19. And as Penelope Gouk has brilliantly shown in this volume [p. 41] and in her many other writings, the same mixture of magic and mechanism may be observed in musical writings of the time. See in particular her book, *Music, Science and Natural Magic in Seventeenth-Century England*, New Haven and London 1999.

mechanical phenomenon as the "trumpet series" produced by overblowing most any brass instrument invites Werckmeister to consider the resulting intervals to constitute a replica of divine creation and the great chain of being. The major / minor duality of harmony that was coming increasingly to the fore in practice inspires in Werckmeister even more rhapsodical musings over the ambivalent nature of man suspended between states of grace and corruption, between poles of the masculine and feminine; while pedantic issues of organ tuning and pipe scaling meander quickly into Pythagorean discourses on the perfection of certain whole numbers and the paradox of having to temper and sully these divine proportions in practice—surely a lesson in the corruption and fall of man since Adam.[20]

Still, Werckmeister cannot be considered typical. He was really one of the last in the line of major *practical* theorists to adopt a universal vision of cosmic *harmonia* in the Boethian sense. Yet for every metaphysical instinct pulling him back towards the Middle Ages, there was also a counter-gravitational pull drawing him forward into the modern era; his awareness and accounts of contemporary music practice were extraordinarily percipient, and he proved to be a pioneer in recognizing and codifying the full transposeable major / minor key system within various tempered chromatic gamuts.

3

Thus by the beginning of the eighteenth century, we can see an important shift in music theory that would henceforth more and more characterize the discipline. On the one hand, those topics that were historically associated with *musica theorica* were becoming relegated to the periphery of the discipline as too speculative and esoteric, or absorbed more innocuously into the nascent disciplines of physical acoustics, mathematics, and later tone psychology. On the other hand, the subjects of *musica practica*, which as we have seen were always considered to be dialectically opposed

---

20. See Andreas Werckmeister, *Musicae mathematicae hodegus curiosus*, Leipzig, 1687, especially pp. 141–54.

to theory, were little by little coming to be understood as "theory". Revealing testimony to this effect is found in Brossard's famous *Dictionnaire de musique* of 1703. There Brossard wrote that properly speaking, a "theorist" was one who was concerned with *théorie*, which is to say, the "simple speculation of an object of an art or science, by which one considers or examines its essence, nature, and properties without regard to its practice" (s.v. "Theoria"). He noted, however, that a number of Italian writers also considered as a *musico theorico* anyone "who has written or given to the public any treatise concerning music, although he is in other respects perhaps an accomplished practician" (s.v. "Theorico"). Still, it was clear that Brossard disapproved of this conflation, since he elsewhere clearly demarcated the genre of "Musica Contemplativa, ou Speculativa, ou Theorica" from "Musica Attiva, ou Prattica", the former dealing with the "reasons of sound, the examination of its nature, properties and effects", the latter with its "execution, without taking into consideration its reasons, nor the causes of its good effect in execution."

As I noted above, some texts in the tradition of canonist *musica theorica* continued to be published through the eighteenth century, including works by Leonhard Euler, Lorenz Mizler, Friedrich Wilhelm Marpurg, and Robert Smith.[21] A very few texts of cosmological harmonics may be found, too.[22] By and large, though, the subject of speculative music theory was not held in high esteem during the high Enlightenment of the eighteenth century. Many of the *philosophes* criticized such writings as symptomatic of the baleful *esprit de système*—the vain fantasies of those scientists and philosophers who construct their systems based not on empirical investigation and moderate induction, but rather by using a priori principles and scholastic methodology. Rameau was widely criticized by many of these *philosophes* for just that reason.

---

21. See footnote 14 for bibliography information on Euler and Marpurg. For Robert Smith, see his *Harmonics or the Philosophy of Musical Sounds* (Cambridge, 1749); for Mizler, see the many articles contained in the journal published for his "Society for Musical Science": *Musikalische Bibliothek,* Leipzig 1736–54.

22. Most notorious, perhaps, is Johann Heinrich Buttstett, *Ut, mi, sol, re, fa, la, Tota Musica et Harmonia Aeterna,* Erfurt c. 1715.

Yet Rameau is ironically the figure who reveals more clearly than any other how Enlightenment philosophy could reconcile theory and practice. The *basse fondamentale*, which is of course the discovery which earned Rameau his fame—and notoriety—as a theorist, is ultimately a brilliant synthesis of theoretical (canonist) traditions with thorough-bass practice. In the first book of his *Traité de l'harmonie* of 1722, Rameau derives (not without some logical slips) the basic harmonies of thorough-bass practice through traditional methods of monochord division. In the subsequent books of his treatise, Rameau goes on to show how the chords he has generated are connected in practice by a small number of cadential progressions that also may be related to their generative source. If Rameau's canonist methods were flawed, they were still based on solid musical intuitions (the notion of a generative chord root and the fundamental priority of the seventh as a dissonance). The result is a tool—the fundamental bass—that is shown to have extraordinarily effective pedagogical value to the teaching of composition and the learning of thorough-bass accompaniment (both intertwined skills in the eighteenth century).[23] As a synthesis, or perhaps more accurately a dialectic, between theoretical rigor and practical empiricism, the *basse fondamentale* is a perfect example not of the *esprit de système*, but of the *esprit systématique*—the measured, inductive systems of philosophy and science that were admired and espoused by the *philosophes*.[24]

Still, this did not protect Rameau from criticism that his theory was still grounded in an outmoded rationalist, not to say virtually gnostic, epistemology. (And to be sure, Rameau was often not his own best defender in these matters.) For Johann Mattheson, perhaps the most severe critic of Rameau, music theory (or "musical mathematics" as he typically called it) was completely at odds with

---

23. For more on Rameau's theory, see my book, *Rameau and Musical Thought in the Enlightenment*, Cambridge 1993. A more succinct account of Rameau's theory is found in Joel Lester, *Compositional Theory in the Eighteenth Century*, Cambridge Mass. 1992, pp. 90–157.
24. I have explored in much greater detail this aspect of Rameau's synthetic method in my book, *Rameau and Musical Thought in the Enlightenment*, especially chapter 2, pp. 21–42.

the aesthetics of galant sensibility and sensationalist psychology of which he was such an ardent champion.[25] But Mattheson was hardly alone; with the triumph of Locke's sensationalist epistemology throughout the continent in the eighteenth century, abstract rationalism and speculative theory was under suspicion by most European intellectuals. In the realm of music, numerous writers advocated Enlightened views of musical empiricism and sentimental aesthetics, including the Germans Friedrich Niedt, Johann David Heinichen, Johann Adolph Scheibe and Johann Philipp Kirnberger; the Encyclopedists Rousseau, d'Alembert and Diderot, and a smattering of theorists from England and Italy.

But a closer examination of this "practical" theory suggests that the issues of their concern were not ones that could be plotted on a theory/practice continuum. That question was not so much one of epistemology and method as it was one of expression. Questions of musical affect and attendant problems of genre, style, and performance became the dominant marker of the musical landscape, one to which music theory as both practice and pedagogy was increasingly subordinated. For questions of musical expression and aural sensibility skew traditional musical divisions, as they cut across both speculative and practical disciplines.[26] While some seventeenth-century writers theorized abstractly (or perhaps "scientifically") about the power of music to arouse emotions (for example, Descartes, Roger North, and Athanasius Kircher), others attempted to show what specific musical tech-

---

25. On Mattheson's empirical aesthetics, see my article, "*Sensus, Ratio,* and *Phthongos*: Mattheson's Theory of Musical Perception", in: Raphael Atlas and Michael Cherlin (eds.), *Musical Intuitions and Transformations: Essays in Honor of David Lewin*, Boston 1994, pp. 1–16.

26. The interest in musical expression and affect is of course a well-known and documented quality of Baroque musical aesthetics. What is perhaps less recognized, though, is how interest in the corporeal effects of music (in its abilities to agitate the passions) seemed to resurrect questions posed already in the Boethian program of *musica humana*. In any case, the obsession of Baroque writers concerning the doctrine of affections (related to interest also in questions of musical sensibility) can be seen as a strong counter-narrative to the traditional theoretical concerns (of speculative theory) with topics of number and form. If we were to propose a third genre of musical theorizing in the Baroque period, it would be less that of "musica poetica" than of "musica affectiva".

niques could be employed in practice to arouse emotions (by choice of mode, rhythmic patterns, rhetorical figures, and so forth). The most comprehensive compositional treatises of the period (such as Heinichen's *Der General-Baß in der Composition* of 1728 or Mattheson's *Der volkommene Capellmeister* of 1739) offered numerous examples of compositional techniques that a musician could employ to generate a specific affect.

If we turn to questions of style, which becomes another dominating concern of Baroque theorists, an even more complex picture emerges, one that again has a destabilizing effect upon the traditional divisions of music theory. As made most famous by Marco Scacchi in the early seventeenth century, there were three prominent styles of musical composition: *musica ecclesiastica*, *musica da camera*, and *musica theatralis*—music for the church, the chamber, and the theater. (The debt to Aristotle's three levels of rhetoric is obvious here.)

But these styles were not exclusively restricted to specific geographic genres, despite their names. For example, "theatrical dissonance" as described by someone like Heinichen could easily be found in works outside of operatic music, just as music in *stile antico* could be found in chamber music. At the same time, national styles of French and Italian music (and to a much lesser degree, "English", "German" or "Polish" music) provided further categories of division that could be layered over the rhetorical divisions of Scacchi. (Composers such as Bach and Handel were commonly celebrated—or sometimes censored—for their penchant to mix all of these styles.) Quite clearly, the terrain of Baroque music was getting quite dense with new categories of style and genre, and these categories could not be easily mapped over traditional theoretical divisions of the musical landscape.

To expand on this last point in a most literal way, consider the illustration shown in Ex. 3. This is from a delightful little book called *Bellum Musicum* by the late seventeenth-century German novelist and musician, Johann Beer.[27] It is a map—literally—of

---

27. Johann Bähr, *Bellum Musicum oder musicalischer Krieg*, 1701. (The orthography of Beer's name varies, and includes Beer, Bähr, Ursus, etc.)

the musical landscape as imagined in Beer's fantastical work, which narrates an allegorical war between musicians led by Queen Composition advocating the newest styles of Italian theatrical music with partisans of more traditional music. But Beer's aesthetic battle is more than a clash of musical styles: it reflects the profound shift to be observed in German Baroque musical thought.

Example 3.: Johann Bähr, *Bellum Musicum oder musicalischer Krieg, in welchem umbständlich erzehlet wird, wie die Königin Compositio nebst ihrer Tochter Harmonia mit denen Hümpern und Stümpern zerfallen und nach beyderseits ergriffenen Waffen zwey blutige Haupt-Treffen sambt der Belagerung der Vestung Systema unfern der Invention-See vorgegangen, auch wie solcher Krieg endlich gestillet und der Friede mit gewissen Grund-Reguln befestigt worden... von Johann Beehren* (1701)

Let us look at a few details of Beer's disciplinary topography. We see that the musical landscape is divided by the kingdoms of double counterpoint in the Northwest, *Figuralia* in the Southeast, and *Choralia* in the Southwest. The region of *Contrapunctus* is the home of such antiquated musical techniques as invertible counterpoint and the canon, conservative genres such as the *fuga* and *passacaglia*, and anachronistic theoretical constructs such as mode, hexachords, solfège, and mensural theory. Lest we miss Beer's opinion on this musical practice, he shows us that this Northwest terrain is nurtured by *Flumen Simplicitatis* and *Dumm* and *Despectus* — interspersed with the lakes of ignorance and contemptibility, and populated with villages called *Schweinsburg, Fressenberg, Sackpfeiffingen, Unverstandingen, Verachtungshofen, Eselbosen, Grob,* and *Stultusberg.*

In contrast, the healthy and sunny territory of *Figuralia* is fed by the lake of invention on the far right of the map — the *Lacus Inventionis* — whose nourishing waters are distributed by rivers with names such as *Mollis* and *Durus, Forte* and *Piano. Figuralia* is the land of progressive musical taste: not only of the newest theatrical genres and styles, but of transposeable key systems, pedagogies of the figured bass, harmonic *inventio*, and accentual metrics. Here we find such wholesome residences as *Gute Weinberg, Concertberg, Tonhofen, Passagio, Orgelberg, Alla Capella, Dorflein Allegro, Semitonia, Quintenberg, Imitationshofen, Fagottburg, Tempo,* and *Saraband*. Note that this terrain is itself divided into two parts: *Terra Instrumentistarum* in the northeast and *Terra Vocalistarum* in the southeast *Ultramontane,* the worlds of chamber and theatrical music, respectively. The more distant land of *Choralia* — church music — seems to have its own reservoir in the foothills of the Southwest with the *Flumen Devotionis.*

The landscape mapped out by Beer, of course, reflects on one level Scacchi's tripartite division of musical styles mentioned above. At the same time, though, it suggests the empirical problems inherent in this triadic system. Note, for instance, how Beer maps instrumental music dangerously between counterpoint and theatrical music, it potentially partaking of both conservative and progressive elements, while the world of Church music seems somewhat detached from the battlefields further north — as if

Church music was somehow innocent of these stylistic tensions. Music theorists should pay special attention to the position of *Vestung Systema*—the Fortress systems, which sits impervious and insulated from the surrounding terrains. In Beer's text, we learn that this fortress is occupied by music scholars and philosophers who spend their days studying ancient music texts, debating the perfection of certain intervals, calculating evermore precise divisions of the monochord, and censoring transgressions of traditional modal theory and counterpoint. They live in other words within their own world of obsolete, abstract systems of speculative philosophy. Significantly, our musical scholastics never come down from their ivory towers to explore the lands surrounding them until a force of invaders led by Queen Composition and Field-Marshall Tactus actually besieges the fortress, burns their treatises, ties them to galley-stocks, and commands them to actually listen to the music of their landsmen. Here is empiricism with a revenge.

There is much more I could say about Beer's hilarious and eye-opening book as a veritable treasure-trove of insight into the musical debates and issues confronting German musicians and music theorists in the late seventeenth century.[28] But what strikes me as most intriguing about Beer's allegory is its seeming subordination of music theory and pedagogy to issues of style. The music-theoretical world is still divided into areas of practical and speculative inquiry, respectively, but only those practical elements relevant to the new tastes of *Musica figuralis* are deemed worthy of study and preservation. The speculative traditions of theoretical study are anachronistically paired with old styles of ecclesiastical music and its theoretical *apparati*—modes, hexachords, mensuration and the like—all to be banished to the deserts of ignorance, the cloisters of the church, and the ivory towers of the academics. For Beer, music theory was something that was mapped out and navigated according to its relevance to practice. And the judgement of its merits was by *sensus*, not *ratio*—a battle cry that would be

---

28. For more on Beer's treatise and its background, see Werner Braun, "Musiksatirische Kriege", in: *Acta Musicologica* 63 (1991), pp. 168–99.

repeated again and again throughout the eighteenth century by similarly empirically-minded writers.

4

I want finally to say something about Dahlhaus's third paradigm of music theory: music analysis. During the seventeenth and eighteenth centuries, examples of music analysis as we might understand the concept today are rare. To be sure, there are some famous examples of "analysis" to be found. In Rameau's *Traité de l'harmonie*, for instance, there is a fundamental-bass analysis of his own fugal motet, "Laboravi clamans". And in the *Nouveau Système* of 1726 there is perhaps the most famous example of eighteenth century "analysis": Rameau's fundamental-bass reading of a recitative from Lully's *Armide*, "Enfin, il est en ma puissance". (This latter example would be discussed by both d'Alembert and Rousseau, and would itself become an object of intense aesthetic debate between Rameau and Rousseau.) A few other selected examples of music analysis between 1650 and 1750 could also be cited.[29] But none of these examples is properly an analysis in the sense discussed by Dahlhaus, which relies on a much later Romantic aesthetic of the musical artwork. Rather than investigating a musical work to reveal its inner content and beauty, these are all *exempla* used by the author for pedagogical purposes to illustrate some pedagogical point or ideal. What is crucially lacking in each of these Baroque *exempla* is a proto-Romantic notion of the autonomous musical artwork deserving and demanding profound contemplation and study by the student. Whereas a music student in the seventeenth or early eighteenth century might study a work of a

---

29. Another early example of musical analysis is discussed by Joel Lester, "An Analysis of Lully from circa 1700", in: *Music Theory Spectrum* 16/1 (1994), pp. 41–61. One of the very earliest "analyses" of music often cited by historians is found in Joachim Burmeister's *Musica poetica* of 1600: a rhetorical parsing of a Lassus motet, "In me transierunt". Again, however, this is analysis is an older sense of *exemplum*. As von Loesch has argued (see footnote 11), the seventeenth-century German writings on *musica poetica* cannot be read as simple anticipations of the nineteenth-century work-concept, with all its attendant aesthetic and social values.

composer for emulation and instruction in his own composition lessons, the Romantic notion of analysis was far less pragmatic. (And given the status of the musical artwork as a monumental and ineffable masterpiece, the idea of strict imitation would have been in any case disputable.) Nineteenth-century critics such as Hoffmann, A.B. Marx, or George Grove would attempt through their analytical hermeneutics to discover the music's inner artistic and spiritual content.[30]

Still, the aesthetic turn of music theory towards issues of style, rhetoric and genre evident in the writings of Mattheson or Scheibe (and adumbrated to a surprising degree by Beer) bespeaks a concern with the poetics of the musical work that could arguably be taken as a foretoken of nineteenth-century music analysis. This concern is made even more explicit in several writings of the Göttingen organist and music historian, Johann Nicolaus Forkel. Known to most musicians today as the first biographer of Bach, Forkel published an important though little-known essay in 1777 under the title "Über die Theorie der Musik".[31] Here for the first time we have music theory used as a disciplinary program we would recognize today—as a synthesis of speculative, practical, and analytic concerns. Arguing that an understanding of music would require a balance of both empirical and rational approaches, Forkel proposed that the true discipline of music theory would incorporate both, much as Kant was shortly to attempt a mediation in his critical philosophy of empiricism and rationalism. In Ex. 4, I have outlined the basics of Forkel's program. Note that parts one and two constitute the traditional and modern domains of speculative harmonics: the mathematical and acoustical study of tone—*Klanglehre*. Part three and four constitute the tradition of systematic theory—the regulation of tonal material in both syntax and form. Here again, Forkel betrays his originality

---

30. For a useful anthology of such nineteenth-century analyses, as well as a revealing discussion of the aesthetics underlying such analyses, see Ian Bent, *Music Analysis in the Nineteenth Century*, 2 vols., Cambridge 1994. Also of value is Dahlhaus's classic monograph, *The Idea of Absolute Music*, translated by Roger Lustig, Chicago 1989.
31. Reprinted in C. F. Cramer's *Magazin der Musik* 1 (1785), pp. 855–912.

Example 4. Johann Forkel, Über die Theorie der Musik *(1777)*

I SPECULATIVE	1. *Die Physikalische Klanglehre*	2. *Die Mathematische Klanglehre*

II REGULATIVE	3. *Die Musikalische Grammatik*	4. *Die Musikalische Rhetorik*
	a. *Zeichenlehre* (notation)	a. *Periodologie* (rhythm and logic)
	b. *Tonarten* (scales, modes and intervals)	b. *Schreibarten* (style)
	c. *Harmonie*	c. *Gattungen* (genre)
	d. *Rhythmopöie*	d. *Anordnung* (composition)
		1. *Aesthetische* (rhetorical divisions)
		2. *Figuren* (figures)
		e. *Vortrag* (performance)

III ANALYTIC	5. *Die Musikalische Kritik*
	a. (On the necessity of rules)
	b. (On beauty)
	c. (Musical taste)

by having recourse to an old discipline-rhetoric—and adapting it creatively as a strategy for analyzing the parts, styles, and genres of music. Performance, as can be seen, is now firmly within the theoretical domain, as it is within the traditional discipline of rhetoric, which considers not only the composition (*inventio*) and structure (*dispositio*) of a speech, but its affect and delivery (*elocutio*).

Interestingly and tellingly, Forkel does not consider style difference as an essential marker. (Again, let me draw attention to contrasts in the structure and style of Forkel's presentation with that of Beer's. The map in Ex. 3 illustrates perfectly, I think, Foucault's *epistēmē* of Renaissance Resemblance.[32] It is based upon principles of affinity and association, and its appearance is regulated by family groups and clusters. Forkel's taxonomy in Ex. 4, however, illustrates Foucault's classical epistemic order of representation. It

---

32. This famous distinction is made in Michel Foucault's *The Order of Things*, London 1972; originally published in 1966 as *Les mots et les choses.*

Genres of Music Theory, 1650–1750

is based upon Enlightenment principles of function and behavior, and its presentation is accordingly tabular and encyclopedic in the model of Petrus Ramus.)

Finally, under part 5, Forkel discusses the role of the critic in evaluating music's beauty, and the necessity for cultivating one's taste in judging musical pieces. Although he does not develop this part of his program in great detail, I think it can be read—as I have suggested above—as a clear foretoken of nineteenth-century music analysis. No longer concerned simply with abstracting and codifying systems of harmony, tonality, counterpoint or meter, let alone in analyzing the numerical or acoustical basis of this material, theorists would turn increasingly to the analysis of individual pieces to deduce norms of practice and standards of worth. (That Forkel himself helped establish Bach's musical works in the canon of Western music during the early nineteenth century affirms that he very much had in mind the kind of autonomous artwork held by Dahlhaus as the aesthetic underpinning of Romantic music analysis.) Of course this aesthetic was not always easily reconciled with the increasing premium the Romantics placed upon creative genius, by which individual masterworks were said to be irreproducible and beyond rational analysis. But it was appropriate that an individual with the historical consciousness of Forkel would see the need to develop tools for the analysis and judgement of musical works. The rise of historicism and of music analysis go hand in hand.

5

This brings us as far as I want to take us on this whirlwind tour of late Baroque music theory, for it has done its duty in introducing us to the complex (and often overlapping) configurations of thought found in this period. Still, it is interesting to see how the basic tripartite division outlined by Dahlhaus provides a useful template for our survey. While a further analysis of the development of music theory in the nineteenth and twentieth centuries would certainly reveal further modifications and reconfigurations of the discipline—particularly with the foundation of systematic musicology by Guido Adler in the late nineteenth century, I am struck by how resilient Dahlhaus's three "genres" remain today, how effectively they continue to serve as coordinates by which to survey our own disciplinary territory. Music theory continues to have a heavily practical orientation, to be sure, as we continue to identify, codify, and classify systems of musical structure and language for music students in our many institutions of musical education. At the same time, music analysis has matured into a lively critical discipline in its own right, although one still heavily tethered to *musica practica* for its pedagogical values. Finally, a seeming resurgence of speculative theory is evident in the writings of several American music theorists, theory that has little ostensible pedagogical or analytic function.[33]

* * *

Music theory has often been said to offer us a lens by which we may hear music — to mix my sensory metaphors. The kinds of languages, models, and questions theory poses help to frame our perceptions and conceptions of music. Yet, to continue my optometrical analogy, there are a multitude of glasses musicians can wear. And over time, we have had occasion to look through many kinds of lenses, many varieties of telescopes and microscopes, since the questions we want to have answered about music have changed, the objects of our scrutiny have shifted.

Of course, theory is usually less spontaneously absorbed than an ocular metaphor suggests. Perhaps a better metaphor is found in the topographical analogies with which I began this talk. Theory can be seen as a set of surveying tools — compass, sextant, plumb line — that produce varieties of maps for our orientation. Its tools might also include microscopes, telescopes, oscilloscopes and radon detectors. Maps vary, as we know, depending upon what it is we might be interested in, what topographical information is deemed important to be recorded. Yet in the history of music theory, I am

---

33. I am thinking here of the work of theorists such as David Lewin, John Clough, and Richard Cohn, all of whom have contributed to the development of neo-Riemannian and "transformational" theory. As in medieval speculative theory, the concern of these theorists is very much with the properties and potential of musical matter. See my contribution "Musicology (Theory)", in the revised *New Grove Dictionary of Music and Musicians*, London 2000.

continually struck by the continuity of thought as I am by the differences. If Dahlhaus's three paradigms of music theory are not exhaustive, they do capture I think on a macro-level three styles of theoretical activity, three genres of map making. Still, within those paradigms, there will always be a need for resurveying the landscape. There will be new settlements to plot, some erosion of the landscape to take into account, and probably even the occasional tectonic shifts in land mass. But while the numbers and kinds of animals we will meet up with in our musical bestiary will always be changing: our need to give them names and some kind of order will probably not.

SCIENCE AND MUSIC, OR THE SCIENCE OF MUSIC: SOME LITTLE-KNOWN EXAMPLES OF "MUSIC THEORY" BETWEEN 1650 AND 1750

Penelope Gouk

The temporal boundaries for this paper, as for our academy, can best be framed with reference to Athanasius Kircher's *Musurgia universalis* (Rome, 1650) on the one hand, and Denis Diderot's *Encylopédie* published between 1751 and 1772 on the other. Both these sources have long been recognized as fundamental texts for Western music theory. The sources to be examined here, however, are not generally known to historians of music theory, even though the subjects they address constituted part of the domain of "music theory" as understood around 1700. What makes these sources doubly remote is that their authors — the physician and Oxford Professor of natural philosophy Thomas Willis (1621–1675), the alchemist and Cambridge Professor of mathematics Isaac Newton (1642–1727), and George Cheyne (1671–1743), the Scottish physician, Newtonian and medical popularizer — are better known to historians of early modern science and medicine. Not one of them, as far as I know, was musically literate, but all were concerned to understand and explain nature in terms of the emerging "new science" of the period, and as we shall see, each had something important to say about music's effects on human nature.[1]

Although not trained in music, they were all university graduates and professional men: Willis and Newton held academic posts for part of their careers, Willis and Cheyne were successful practising physicians, while both Newton and Cheyne taught mathematics.

---

1. This paper develops some of the key themes discussed in Penelope Gouk, "The Role of Harmonics in the Scientific Revolution", in: Thomas Christensen (ed.), *The Cambridge History of Western Music Theory*, Cambridge 2002, pp. 223–45.

In other words, they had qualifications in mathematics and natural philosophy, and it was in this intellectual context that they came to write about music in ways that I hope to show are particularly relevant to the "new science" that became established during their lifetimes, and especially as this experimentally-based practice came to be understood in British culture.

The domain of practical music was one of the most important resources for seventeenth-century natural philosophers who sought to know the world experimentally, to discover the mathematical laws and hidden harmonies that governed the universe, and to establish a new, more effective scientific method that built on reliable sensory data. The crucial difference was that now, for the first time, "science", just like music, was becoming increasingly understood in terms of its *practice* rather than simply denoting a theoretical system.[2] The Scientific Revolution is now generally defined as the period when science, or natural philosophy, first became identified with advancing knowledge and control of the natural world, most notably through the mathematisation of physics.[3] Today the application of mathematics to the physical world, experimental observation, and the manipulation of natural forces are seen as hallmarks of the scientific method, as was already the case in Diderot's enlightened age.

However, before the seventeenth century, and even well into it, these defining characteristics of science were more associated with natural magic—that is (according to definitions of the time) the art of bringing about amazing effects by using hidden, insensible and inanimate forces in nature. Although the rejection of magic is traditionally one of the defining features of the Scientific Revolution, many aspects of natural magic, most notably the use of instruments to extend the range and power of the human senses, and to cause powerful effects at a distance, were simply

---

2. H. F. Cohen, *Quantifying Music: The Science of Music at the First Stage of the Scientific Revolution, 1580–1650*, Dordrecht 1984; Penelope Gouk, *Music, Science and Natural Magic in Seventeenth-Century England*, New Haven and London 1999, especially pp. 7–14; Paolo Gozza (ed.), *Number to Sound: The Musical Way to the Scientific Revolution*, Dordrecht 2000.
3. John Henry, *The Scientific Revolution and the Origins of Modern Science*, Houndsmills and London 1997.

taken over by, and absorbed into, experimental philosophy.[4] My contention is that musical instruments were among the most important, yet historically most neglected, devices which transformed early modern Europeans' ways of knowing and understanding the world.

MUSIC AND EXPERIMENT: MAGIC, SCIENCE, AND THE "NEW PHILOSOPHY"

The principal reason why musical models were central to the development of a new kind of "scientific" thinking was that the first quantitative laws to be discovered in the seventeenth century were those we now call Mersenne's laws, since it was Marin Mersenne (1588–1648) who experimentally determined the relationship between length, tension and cross-sectional area of a vibrating string and its frequency.[5] By 1650 these harmonic laws were already providing a model for natural philosophers like Descartes, who sought to establish similar laws in other branches of the physical sciences, and the same search was later made by Robert Hooke and Isaac Newton in the later seventeenth century. As is well known, these harmonic laws built on the discovery attributed to Pythagoras, namely the arithmetic relationship between string length and frequency, a musical law which provided the grounds for the strict distinction between consonance and dissonance found in Boethius's *De musica*.

However, there were important differences between this traditional harmonic division and the new harmonic laws of Mersenne. The first difference was that Mersenne derived his laws from extensive investigation into the many different variables affecting pitch, not just those in musical strings but also those found in pipes and other sounding bodies. Musical instruments provided Mersenne with experimental apparatus for investigating many different properties of sound, a quest which effectively turned musical instruments into philosophical, or "scientific" instru-

---

4. Henry, op.cit.; also Gouk, *Music, Science and Natural Magic*, chapters 3 and 5.
5. Cohen, *Quantifying Music*, pp. 97–114; Gouk, *Music, Science and Natural Magic*, pp. 170–8.

ments, in that they were artifically manipulated in order to yield new knowledge (by way of contrast to their primary function of making music).

The second way Boethius's musical rule differed from Mersenne's was that Boethius sought the explanation of consonance in the perfection of the first four integers. By contrast, Mersenne located the source of music's power in actual sound, the subject of acoustics, the new experimental discipline that the English philosopher and Lord Chancellor Francis Bacon first identified in the 1620s. Specifically, Mersenne had a theory of consonance which has retrospectively been called the "coincidence theory" because it says that intervals are more or less pleasing according to the relative frequency at which the pulses of musical sound coincide, as they strike the ear. Mersenne thought that the power of music stems from the similarity between sound waves and the motion that is imprinted on the eardrum, an action that creates a corresponding motion in the animal spirits that flow through the nerves, which in turn stimulate the vital spirits in the blood to move towards or away from the heart, the seat of the passions.

Mersenne's explanation of consonance proved pertinent to the new mechanical philosophy that was being developed by Descartes as an alternative to Aristotelianism, a unified system in which all phenomena, from the motion of planets to people's emotions, might be explained mechanistically in terms of moving particles of matter.[6] However, although all three of my British natural philosophers also took matter in motion as their starting-point for explaining music's effects, their approach resembled Bacon's concept of a new inductive method more than Descartes's rigorously deductive system. Francis Bacon (1561–1626) was a key figure in the process whereby natural magic was absorbed into, and eventually taken over by, experimental science, and his legacy can be seen in the three authors whose work I am focusing on here. This transformation, or appropriation, of magic can be demonstrated particularly effectively with reference to the new dicipline

---

6. Claude V. Palisca, "Moving the Affections through Music: Pre-Cartesian Psycho-Physiological Theories", in: Gozza, *Number to Sound*, pp. 289–308.

of acoustics for which Bacon mapped out a preliminary experimental agenda that was enthusiastically taken up by Mersenne and other natural philosophers in the seventeenth century.

Bacon's experimental science of acoustics was both a practical art — which included the construction of instruments that could imitate natural sounds and create artificial harmonies — and also a theoretical science, which he identified as a "higher kind of natural magic". Bacon rejected the notion that music (i.e. harmony) is explained by arithmetic ratios, which by themselves tell us nothing about the lived experience of music. Rather than taking refuge in Pythagorean numbers, Bacon advised his followers (using modern terminology here for a moment) to take a phenomenological approach in this new science of sound, so that attention would be focused on the qualities of the sounds produced by different musical instruments, and their capacity to create harmony. His was a science that would seek to investigate how different modes and musical genres seem to move people differently (which may be according to their individual or national temperament), and which sought to explore parallels between bodily instruments and organs and man-made instruments.

THE POWER OF SYMPATHY

Bacon believed that a crucial starting-point in all these investigations (or "Experiments", as he called them) was to focus on sympathy, the capacity of musical bodies to resonate with each other, for example in the case of a lute one string that has been set in motion is able to set another string in motion (maybe on another instrument altogether) by virtue of an occult power about which conventional scholastic physics literally had nothing to say. As taught in medieval universities, scholastic physics only concerned itself with phenomena that were manifest to the senses and which could be described in qualitative terms. Musical sympathy was by definition an occult phenomenon, in that its causes were hidden rather than manifest, and therefore according to scientific standards of the time these causes were unknowable, that is, unintelligible. The starting-point of natural magic was that although the causes of a particular phenomenon might be inexplicable, it was nevertheless a real effect whose actions could be demonstrated. In Bacon's lifetime, that is around 1600, the phenomenon of musical sympathy was the archetypal example of natural magic. This canonic status was partly due to resonance between musical strings being a marvellous effect that could easily be demonstrated with the appropriate apparatus (e.g. two lutes, two theorbos), and as is well known it is precisely this period when instruments with sympathetic strings began to come into fashion at European courts. The other reason why musical resonance became an emblem of natural magic was because the "occult philosophy", as natural magic increasingly came to be known, was assumed to operate according to the hidden harmonies of nature, its starting-point being the assumption that the microcosm and the macrocosm are connected by virtue of hidden sympathies, and the true magus is one who knows how to manipulate these sympathies, as well as understand their causes.[7]

Among the occult forces that appeared to work at great distances which Bacon identified as deserving further enquiry were magnetism and gravity. In Bacon's animistic conception of the universe, which assumed everything was made up of a combination of spirit and matter, these attractive powers were scarcely different in kind from the effects that could be achieved by virtue of one person's spirit and force of imagination acting on another's spirit and imagination by invisible, but nevertheless still effective, means. Music's power to move the passions strongly (a goal which composers like Monteverdi had only recently begun to articulate) and to which Bacon ascribed an affinity between the human spirit and the movement of organized musical sound, was perhaps the most vivid instance of this magic in operation, the musician being a natural magician *par excellence*.[8]

---

7. In addition to Gouk, *Music, Science and Natural Magic*, see also Gary Tomlinson, *Music in Renaissance Magic: Toward a Historiography of Others*, Chicago and London 1993.
8. Graham Rees, "Francis Bacon's Semi-Paracelsian Cosmology and the Great Instauration", in *Ambix* 22 (1975), pp. 81–101; D.P. Walker, "Francis Bacon and *Spiritus*", reprinted in: D.P. Walker, *Music, Spirit and Language in the Renaissance*, London 1985; Gouk, *Music, Science and Natural Magic*, pp. 158–170.

Science and Music, or the Science of Music

As well as Bacon's science of acoustics, the archetypal instance of this overlap between sympathetic magic, music and experiment is found in works by the English physician and Rosicrucian Robert Fludd (1574–1637), whose *History of the Macrocosm and Microcosm* (1617–21) was the first printed work to include pictorial representations of cosmic and human harmony based on the principles of Neoplatonism.[9] The crucial element of these illustrations is their use of musical instruments or parts of instruments, especially the vibrating string, as a means of conceptualising how matter and non-matter, bodies and minds, interact with each other, both at the level of the macrocosm (i.e. the universe and the planets) and the microcosm (i.e. the inner workings of the human mind and its effect on the body) by means of sympathy. The idea that all parts of the universe are sympathetically related, and that an action carried out in one part of the universe can have an effect at another was especially easy to grasp in musical terms.

In short, thanks to Fludd, Mersenne (who disagreed with Fludd although he believed in universal harmony), and also Kircher, whose *Musurgia universalis* was accessible in every corner of the known world, the image of the cosmos as a divine monochord, God's instrument, became a commonplace of seventeenth-century thought, exactly the way that the body of man, the microcosm, was also imagined as a musical instrument.[10] These musical analogies clearly went to the heart of mid-seventeenth century debates about the nature of bodies, the nature of souls, and the hidden forces that govern the interaction of matter and spirit. Indeed, I want to go further and argue that these musical models, although they clearly overlap with, and complement, mechanical models (e.g. the universe as a watch or the body as a hydraulic organ), offered something that other analogies couldn't provide.

The reason why musical models had such power is that the analogy doesn't just rely on how the instrument works. The point

---

9. Joscelyn Godwin, *Robert Fludd: Hermetic Philosopher and Surveyor of Two Worlds*, London 1979.
10. Penelope Gouk, "Making Music, Making Knowledge: The Harmonious Universe of Athanasius Kircher", in: Daniel Stolzenberg (ed.), *The Great Art of Knowing: The Baroque Encylopaedia of Athanasius Kircher*, Stanford 2001, pp. 71–83.

about musical instruments is that they have to be played with intention in order for music to be made, for its effects to be communicated and experienced. And at the core of that experience is "sympathy", a mysterious phenomenon that cannot be explained simply in terms of matter touching matter, but is an action that works incorporeally and even at a great distance. The crucial thing is that although sympathy is mysterious (i.e difficult to explain rationally and discursively), it really exists, and music is one of the ways in which it can be known experimentally.

As the rest of my paper demonstrates, this fundamental insight was used to good effect by each of the authors whose work I am considering here, not only for conceptualising the hidden mechanisms of mind-body interaction, but for imagining how these were analogous to more fundamental interactions within the cosmic system. Although not part of the music theory that is normally studied by students of the discipline, I hope to show that this "speculative" material (and much more like it) deserves further investigation by those who want to understand what music meant to people in the so-called Baroque era.

THOMAS WILLIS ON "MUSICAL EARS"

Thomas Willis was a successful medical practitioner who was also the Professor of Natural Philosophy at the University of Oxford (1660–1675). In the annals of medicine he is famous as the founder of a new discipline of neurophysiology, based on a rigorous experimental method and acute observation of the structure of the brain and nervous system. In short, he exemplifies the new, "scientific" medicine which was emerging in the seventeenth century, especially as an early member of the Royal Society (founded 1660) and a participant in the proto-scientific research groups active in the decades before its foundation.[11]

Willis is not known to have been a musician himself, his closest connection to music being the fact that he was Roger North's

---

11. Robert G. Frank, *Harvey and the Oxford Physiologists: Scientific Ideas and Social Interaction*, Berkeley, Los Angeles and London 1980; Michael Hunter, *The Royal Society and Its Fellows: The Morphology of an Early Scientific Institution*, Oxford² 1994.

physician. (North was an accomplished musical amateur who wrote extensively on all aspects of music theory, but none of this material was printed before the nineteenth century and consequently it had no influence during our period.)[12] The reason Willis's name is connected with music is because he was the first medical author to discuss the concept of "musical ears". The relevant passage is found in Willis's *De Cerebri anatome* which was first published in Latin in 1664, but had been translated into English as the "Anatomy of the Brain and Nervous System" by 1683.[13] Apart from talking about "musical ears", the book laid the foundations for a new discipline of neurology (another new term Willis coined, together with "reflex action"), and remained required reading on this subject until the middle of the nineteenth century.

One of the most interesting aspects of Willis's neurological observations for the history of science is that they are framed within a theory of active matter which combines both chemical and mechanical properties; in other words he is closer to Bacon's universe of *spiritus* mingling with matter than to Descartes's cosmos of inert matter in which all phenomena are explained in terms of contact action.[14] And as Jamie Kassler has argued in her book *Inner Music*, Willis's model of the body is also musical in that it is implicitly based on the *hydraulis*, in other words an automatic organ powered by both wind and water.[15]

From the perspective of music theory, the most interesting thing about Willis's concept of musical ear is how it was immediately taken up by Thomas Salmon in his *Essay to the Advancement of Music* (1672), which opens with the statement that

---

12. Mary Chan and Jamie C. Kassler (eds.), *Roger North's The Musicall Grammarian 1728*, Cambridge 1990; Jamie C. Kassler, *Inner Music: Hobbes, Hooke and North on Internal Character*, London 1995.
13. Thomas Willis, "The Anatomy of the Brain and Nerves", in: Thomas Willis, *The Remaining Medical Works*, London 1683, pp. 118–20.
14. Penelope Gouk, "Some English Theories of Hearing in the Seventeenth Century: Before and after Descartes", in: Charles Burnett, Michael Fend, and Penelope Gouk (eds.), *The Second Sense: Studies in Hearing and Musical Judgement from Antiquity to the Seventeenth Century*, London 1991, pp. 95–113.
15. Jamie C. Kassler, "Blowing the Organ: Willis, Hydro-Pneumatics and Hierarchy", in: Jamie C. Kassler, *Music, Science, Philosophy: Models in the Universe of Thought*, Aldershot 2001, pp. 125–64.

> God hath created a particular faculty of hearing to recieve harmonious sounds, clearly different from that by which we perceive ordinary noises. ... those who have not this musical hearing, are by nature, as uncapable to understand Harmony, as a Horse is to receive the civility of a compliment ... here is some specific power which sub-divides this more private faculty from the common nature of hearing ... but whether the distinction comes from a different formation of the little intrigues of the ear, or only from an improvement of some men's souls are able to make of sounds so qualified and represented to them, it is hard to determine.[16]

Salmon tells readers again about this "specific power" in the *Vindication of an Essay* (also published in 1672) where he defends his novel theories from the scorn of Matthew Locke. Here Salmon cites chapter 17 of Willis's *Cerebri* with reference to "some peculiar schematism of the Cerebellum" that may determine people's receptivity to music.[17]

In brief, the immediate context for Willis's observation that "some have musical ears, and others are wholly destitute of that faculty" is a discussion of the seventh pair of nerves, the auditory nerves. The softer nerve of the pair Willis thinks is responsible for the sensation of hearing, while the harder one "seems to perform some motions". He notes that this latter nerve is divided into three branches which are carried "without the Skull" (i.e. outside it), all of which serve to "pathetic motions, or at least to such are performed without consulting the brain"; in other words they are responsible for involuntary actions.[18]

Willis goes on to discuss how these three branches are implicated when animals, on hearing a sudden impulse or loud noise, immediately prick up their ears, open their eyes, and cry out. A comparable set of (reflex) actions can be observed in humans, who often cry out involuntarily when exposed to an unaccustomed or

---

16. Thomas Salmon, *An Essay to the Advancement of Musick, by Casting Away the Perplexities of Different Cliffs*, London 1672, p. 2.
17. Thomas Salmon, *A Vindication of an Essay to the Advancement of Musick, from Mr Matthew Locke's Observations*, London 1672, p. 34.
18. These and all following extracts are taken from the English version of Willis's *Anatomy of the Brain*, chapter 17, "Of the Nerves Serving the involuntary Function", pp. 117–9.

horrible noise. However, Willis thinks that the division of the auditory nerves serves a further purpose in mankind, which is that the voice can "fitly answer to the hearing", in other words it can respond to the sound heard like an echo. The difference between this vocal response and a "common" (i.e. real) echo is that the latter is an immediate reflection of the original sound, while in humans there can be a delay before the reflected sound is carried out through the mouth, one which also may not be exactly the same as the original.

Willis explains this disjuncture by a materialist theory of mind, in which each mental faculty (e.g. common sense, reason, imagination, memory) is physically located in a particular ventricle of the brain, and all mental operations are carried out through the activity of the animal spirits that flow like wind through the nerves and the substance of the brain. It should be understood that Willis identified these spirits as the sensitive soul, one that was possessed by man as well as other animals. He thought of this soul as a fiery, aery and vital substance that is corporeal and chemical in nature, but which serves as the agent of the immaterial, rational soul. In sum, the sensitive soul is the means by which voluntary as well as involuntary actions in the body are executed.[19] Not coincidentally, this mysterious substance which mediates between matter and non-matter, between body and soul, and which has a special affinity with music, also appears in the texts by Newton and Cheyne to be considered below.[20]

First, however, let us return to Willis and his explanation of human responses to sound. An unusual aspect of Willis's faculty psychology was his claim that memory has two "distinct Storehouses" rather than only one. The "Brain" (that is, the cerebrum)

---

19. This is developed in Thomas Willis, "Two Discourses Concerning the Soul of Brutes", in his *Remaining Medical Works*, London 1683, first published as Thomas Willis, *De anima brutorum quae hominis vitalis ac sensitiva est, exercitationes duae*, Oxford 1672.
20. D. P. Walker, "Medical Spirits in Philosophy and Theology from Ficino to Newton", reprinted in: Walker, *Music, Spirit and Language*. See also Gouk, "Music, Melancholy and Medical Spirits in Early Modern Thought", in: Peregrine Horden (ed.), *Music as Medicine: The History of Music Therapy since Antiquity*, Guilford 2000, pp. 173–94.

is the 'Chest of memory' which stores artificial or acquired memories, while the "Cerebel" (that is, the cerebellum) is the place of "natural memory". Thus the delayed "echo" effect in humans, where the original sound is belatedly mirrored by the voice, is the result of the sound impressions going into the Cerebel before they move outwards to the mouth again. It seems that the "Idea" of the sound originally heard can stay in the head, until "as occasion serves" the voice is formed, a sound which bears the "image" of the original, even though this was heard some time before.

At last this brings us to Willis's digression on why some people are more musical than others, which elaborates on his theory of natural and artificial memory. As already explained, the audible impulse is carried by the animal spirits along the nerves to the "common sensory … and being also delivered to the Brain, stirs up the Imagination [which is also located in the cerebrum], and so leaves in its Cortex an image or private mark of it self for the [artificial] Memory." At the same time, however, the Ideas of the Sounds are also conveyed to the Cerebel, the seat of innate memory, where they form footsteps or tracts, and impress a "remembrance of themselves" in its soft substance.

It may be, therefore, that people who find it difficult to repeat a melody they have heard, suffer from their Cerebel being too hard, which means that music will literally fail to make an impression on them! Accordingly the species move on to the Brain and leave their traces there, but since this is still busy with other motions it is "less apt to keep distinctly the composures of Harmony". By contrast, people who have an impressionable Cerebel can reproduce, or "bring forth with exact Symphony" a melody they have heard, because the spirits flow into the footsteps of the original sound and become organized like them, so that "like a Machine or Clock with the succession of Species, the measures or Tunes of the Instrument which they had drunk in at the ears". A similar expla-

---

19. Günter Grass, *From the Diary of a Snail*, trans. Ralph Manheim (London: Minerva, 1997). First published as *Aus dem Tagebuch einer Schnecke* in 1972.
20. Dominique Jameux, *Pierre Boulez*, trans. Susan Bradshaw (London: Faber & Faber, 1991), p. 364.

nation is offered for music's power to allay "all turbulent passions" excited in the breast through the blood becoming overheated: the spirits that have been impressed with music go on to compose the spirits in the breast "to numbers and measures of dancing, and so appeases all tumults and inordinations therein excited."[21]

Here the foundations are laid for eighteenth-century British theories about a good ear for music.[22] On the one hand this ability is something inborn, namely a highly sensitive soul and a receptivity to musical harmony, patterns of sound that reorganize part of the brain and allow one to make music. The implication being, of course, that if you are not born with the right kind of sensitivity, then you are dull and a "Fool at Music". Yet this materialist theory also allows for a developmental model, the argument being that if you do play and listen to music enough then gradually your cerebellum will get tracks laid down in it, and your nerves will become more responsive and more sensitive — a quality which became an essential precondition for the eighteenth-century cult of sensibility.[23]

ISAAC NEWTON AND OCCULT VIBRATING MATTER

Isaac Newton has been an icon of "modern science" since the Enlightenment. This was because he was the first philosopher to offer a grand unified theory of the universe in his *Principia mathematica* or *Mathematical Principles of Natural Philosophy* (London 1687), where it is demonstrated that all bodies from planets to apples are subject to the same universal laws of gravitational attraction. In this work Newton doesn't try to explain the "causes" of this occult attraction working at a distance. Rather, he was able

---

21. Willis, *Anatomy*, p. 118.
22. Notably Frances Hutcheson, *An Inquiry into the Original of Our Ideas of Beauty and Virtue*, London 1725; and Charles Avison, *An Essay on Musical Expression*, London 1752.
23. George S. Rousseau, "Nerves, Spirits and Fibres: Towards Defining the Origins of Sensibility", in: R.F.B. Issenden and J.C. Eade (eds.), *Studies in the Eighteenth Century III*, Canberra 1976; also Anne C. Vila, *Enlightenment and Pathology: Sensibility in the Literature and Medicine of Eighteenth-Century France*, Baltimore and London 1998.

to analyse it mathematically, so that the behaviour of planets and falling bodies could be represented and predicted, and reduced to mathematical and mechanical principles.[24] This was a method his contemporaries admired, and hoped to apply to all aspects of the world, Rameau's application of it to the principles of music being a notable case in point.[25]

As I have elaborated in detail elsewhere, there were three key areas in which Newton's understanding of music (harmony) laid the groundwork for eighteenth-century science, namely optics, wave mechanics, and the laws of universal gravitation.[26] However, there is a further part to this story of Enlightenment that is relevant here, in that Newton also proved to be the source of more speculative thinking about the nature of life and matter that circulated in the eighteenth century, as a result of some of the things he had written in sections of his publications that took the form of "Scholia" (notes amplifying a proof or course of reasoning, as in mathematics) and "Queries" that were deliberately separated from the things he was confident about.

This "speculative" material turns out to be the legacy of Newton's obsession with alchemy, biblical exegesis and other occult subjects that he kept private, a self-censorship he imposed because of their potentially dangerous and heretical nature. Even after his death the full extent of Newton's commitment to these subjects remained unknown until the late twentieth century.[27] Nevertheless, these "speculative" ideas (which by implication lack rigour and have nothing to do with science) had a distinct and measurable impact on eighteenth-century thought, which leads me to suggest that we are looking at things the wrong way round

---

24. For an introduction to the extensive literature on Newton, see John Fauvel et al. (eds.), *Let Newton Be! A New Perspective on His Life and Works*, Oxford 1988.
25. Thomas Christensen, *Rameau and Musical Thought in the Enlightenment*, Cambridge 1993.
26. Gouk, "Harmonics in the Scientific Revolution", pp. 235–39. See also my article "The Harmonic Roots of Newtonian Scienc" in: *Let Newton Be!*, pp. 101–25, and chapter seven of *Music, Science and Natural Magic*.
27. For a reassessment, see Betty Jo Teeter Dobbs, *The Foundations of Newton's Alchemy*, Cambridge 1975.

if we simply dismiss speculative harmonics in that period as a "venerable, if largely enfeebled" subject.[28]

In this paper, I want to revisit Newton's optical material, with a view to considering its relevance as an essential reference point for later medical and scientific understandings of perception and mind-body interaction, theories in which musical models apparently still had an important role to play. In particular I want to emphasize Newton's commitment to maintaining an animating, divine principle in a universe which is harmonically constructed, because it is this dynamic, vital quality of music as immaterial, yet highly organized sound in motion, that makes it such a valuable conceptual resource in contexts where both words and vision fail.

Newton's theory of a seven-fold division of the spectrum (i.e. the seven colours of the rainbow and its resemblance to the seven tones of the musical scale) was first made public in the *Opticks* (1704). This contained the fruits of research that Newton conducted between the mid 1660s and mid 1670s, when he was a young Professor of Mathematics at Trinity College, Cambridge. During this decade Newton was also passionately involved in alchemical research, an activity that was very definitely not part of his job, but a secret experimental practice that formed part of his extra-curricular pursuit of God's hidden truths. The main reason why the *Opticks* wasn't published earlier was because Newton had failed to come up with a satisfactory unified theory of light. However, even when the *Opticks* finally did see publication it was still theoretically flawed, in that the mathematics presented in Book 1 and Book 2 implicitly relied on two very different physical models of light propagation.[29]

In brief, the first part of the *Opticks* assumes that light consists of minute particles, all of the same size and shape, which are constantly emitted from luminous bodies in all directions. With this kinetic or "billiard ball" model taken from Descartes, properties like reflection and refraction can be explained in terms of these

---

28. As claimed by Burdette Green and David Butler in the opening paragraph of their chapter "From acoustics to *Tonpsychologie*" in: Christensen (ed.), *History of Western Music Theory*, p. 246.
29. Gouk, *Music, Science and Natural Magic*, pp. 237–46.

light particles changing speed and direction when they strike a surface. However, this model (which also underpins the section in the *Principia* that treats light and sound as fluid dynamics) could not be used to mathematise most properties of light, especially its periodic qualities. It is no coincidence that Newton in this first part of the book says nothing about the seven-fold division of the spectrum, which takes for granted that light is periodic in nature.

It is in Book 2 of the *Opticks* that the spectrum-scale analogy first appears, an analogy which proves to be inseparable from the second, alternative physical model of light that underpins this part of Newton's work. In other words, it is by virtue of adopting a specifically musical analogy that Newton had fruitful insights into the nature of light. This theory is known as "fits of easy reflexion and transmission" because it assumes that light particles are of different masses and excite condensations and rarefactions in the medium they have to pass through as they move from the luminous body (e.g. the sun) towards the surfaces of other bodies. These periodic condensations and rarefactions set up in the medium are responsible for alternately reflecting and transmitting the light particles, a theory which explains refrangibility, a phenomenon that Newton links to the sensation of different colours that are excited in the eye when vibrations of different wavelengths strike the retina and are transmitted via the optic nerves to the brain.

Newton presented his comparison between musical harmonies and colour harmonies in the *Opticks* as though it were nothing more than an interesting conjecture, tucked away in a series of "Queries" (especially numbers 13 and 14) at the end of the volume. So here we find him casually suggesting that light rays produce sensations of different colours according to their refrangibility, and therefore just as certain combinations of musical tones strike us as either harmonious or discordant, so certain combinations of colours are pleasing or disagreeable depending on the proportions of the vibrations "propagated through the fibres of the optick [nerve]".[30]

---

30. Newton, *Opticks* (1704), p. 136.

What Newton doesn't make explicit is that the mathematics in Book 2 *actually requires this conjecture* to be true: in other words the existence of an extremely fine and elastic medium that interacts with light particles is an essential basis for the "certain" part of this work, rather than merely a "speculative" add-on tacked on to something he has already arrived at by more orthodox means. Another thing Newton doesn't mention is the route by which he arrived at this musical insight, which was a consequence of another natural philosopher criticising his ideas. This was none other than Robert Hooke, the Royal Society's Curator of Experiments, who was among the first to read Newton's account of the prism experiments that led to his discovery of the composite nature of white light, sent in a letter by Newton to the Secretary of the Royal Society in 1672.[31]

I won't go into the details of Hooke's criticisms here, except to point out that the letter he penned in response to Newton's discovery included two important suggestions: first, that Newton's corpuscular theory could not account for all the optical phenomena it was supposed to explain; and second, that colour and musical tone are intimately related to each other by virtue of their vibrational, periodic nature. It is no coincidence that Newton started to weave musical comparisons into his physical theory of colour after receiving Hooke's detailed analysis of its shortcomings.

The musical analogy that Newton began to explore in 1672 eventually came to play a central role in his ethereal explanation of colour perception. He first made this public in "An Hypothesis explaining the properties of light" sent to the Royal Society in December 1675. In this Newton now explained all optical phenomena in terms of the interaction of light corpuscles of varying mass and an extremely fine material ether, which he thought might also be the source of other hidden powers in nature, including gravity. We now know that Newton's conception of this universal ether was modelled on the vital, animating principle of nature, or *spiritus*, of which the alchemists spoke, by which God

---

31. Gouk, *Music, Science and Natural Magic*, pp. 215–8.

moulded the universe to his providential design. Newton didn't say so in the "Hypothesis", but the properties invested in the ether that he describes betray its alchemical and magical origins. This new ether theory allowed Newton to have light particles and also to explain their wave-like properties. He was now in a position to suggest that the sensations of different colours are produced in a similar way to musical tones, in a passage which recalls the first Queries in the *Opticks*, and ends with the observation that

> possibly colour may be distinguisht into its principall Degrees, Red, Orange, Yellow, Green, Blew, Indigo, and deep violett, on the same ground, that Sound within an eighth is graduated into tones.[32]

At this point in the "Hypothesis" Newton introduces his "discovery" that the length of the spectrum can be divided up into ratios corresponding with the musical scale, presenting it as though he discovered this by experiment. In fact, as Newton admits elsewhere, it happened the other way around, in that he tried out the musical division to see if it fitted on an ad hoc basis, a manoeuvre that required him to add indigo and orange to the five main colours he actually saw in the first place.

To recap, then, by the mid 1670s Newton was able to explain the nature of colour and its perception most effectively when he compared it to harmony, and at the same time assumed the existence of a vital ether that filled the universe. Yet during the 1680s while he was working on the *Principia* Newton dropped the ether hypothesis altogether, and moved towards the theory of universal attraction as an alternative explanatory principle. Thus in the *Principia* Newton simply assumes that gravity is an attractive principle of unknown cause, and shows the mathematical laws that can describe its properties. No mention is made here of the spectrum-scale analogy, and light is treated simply as the motion of identically-sized particles moving through space.

---

32. H.W. Turnbull (ed.), *The Correspondence of Isaac Newton*, 7 vols., Cambridge 1959–77, I, p. 376.

Newton's ideas were to change, however, and during the late 1680s and early 1690s when he began preparing his optical papers for publication, this musical analogy and the ether associated with it resurfaced once more. During this period he was also planning to produce a second edition of the *Principia* which would have included additional material in the form of Scholia that explained his theories of matter, space and gravitation. In the end, this projected new edition never appeared.

However, Newton continued to mull over the nature of matter, and the hidden forces and harmonies of nature. Some of these speculations were added to the second English edition of the *Opticks* (1717), including Queries 22, 23 and 24, in which we can finally see the essential connection between Newton's theories of planetary and human motion. In Query 22 Newton asks his readers to imagine an incredibly dense yet subtle medium that fills the universe and which is seven hundred times more elastic and seven hundred times more rare than air. Query 23 goes on to suggest that both vision and sound may be performed by the vibrations of this (or some other) medium which excite the optic and auditory nerves. These motions are propagated through the "solid, pellucid and uniform Capillamenta of those Nerves into the place of Sensation".[33] Newton doesn't attempt to describe the physiology of sensation and perception, but he clearly assumes that regular, proportional vibrations are the basis for the perception of both colour and musical harmonies.

Indeed, Query 24 explicitly asks readers to consider whether animal motion might also be performed by the vibrations of a medium which Newton has already suggested may fill the entire universe. Specifically, he suggests that this medium may serve to perform the actions of the will, first having being excited in the brain and then propagated from thence into the nerves and muscles, which then contract or dilate accordingly. In other words the medium is similar to, if not identical with, Willis's sensitive soul, a fiery and vital substance that serves as the agent of the rational soul. In Newton's model, however, the nerves are solid and

---

33. Newton, *Opticks* (1704), p. 328.

uniform, rather than pipes, and the motion of this aetherial medium is propagated uniformly along them, ideally without interruption since obstructions create palsies (namely inability to move a body part or loss of muscle control).

In conclusion to this section on Newton, and by way of introduction to Cheyne, we can see that the author of the *Principia* was no mechanist, if by this we mean someone who wants to exclude God as an explanatory principle from nature and conceives its operation in purely mechanical terms. Rather, he envisaged the universe as God's sensorium, and the universal aether or *spiritus* as the vehicle through which He exercises his divine will, just as the animal spirits in the brain and nervous system serve as the vehicle for the human will. At the same time, however, Newton also gave grounds for thinking that the harmonic laws of nature are to be discovered operating within the human frame, perhaps to be found in the motions of the nerves themselves, or in the fluid which flows through them, in the manner of stringed or wind instruments that are animated by vibration.

GEORGE CHEYNE ON "WELL-TUNED" NERVES

My final examples of musical models being used to understand the hidden workings of cosmic and human bodies are taken from the prolific writings of George Cheyne (c. 1671–1743), a Scottish physician educated at Edinburgh who spent most of his medical career in London and Bath — the latter being a spa town where he attended wealthy patrons trying to recover from the excesses of luxurious living.[34] Cheyne is notable as one of the first doctors in the eighteenth century to ascribe most diseases to disorders of the nerves, rather than concentrating on the imbalance of humours. So, for example, in his best-selling work *The English Malady, Or a Treatise of Nervous Diseases of all Kinds in Three Parts* (London 1733), instead of melancholy being caused by an excess of black bile or choler (hence the term melancholia), Cheyne ascribes it to

---

34. Anita Guerrini, *Obesity and Depression in the Enlightenment: The Life and Times of George Cheyne*, Norman 2000.

a poor state of the nerves and the animal spirits which flow through them. After 1750 this nervous pathology became increasingly part of mainstream medicine, so by the time Thomas Trotter published *A View of the Nervous Temperament* in 1807, Britain was apparently in the grip of a veritable epidemic of diseases (including melancholy and the related afflictions of hysteria and hypochondria) that were caused by the poor state of (middle-class) people's nerves.[35]

An earlier best-seller by Cheyne was *The Essay of Health and Long Life* (London 1724), a work that had its origins in the instructions that a wealthy patient asked Cheyne to draw up on his departure to Bath "in order to direct him in the conduct of his health for the future". Cheyne willingly supplied these rules, and to make his book accessible to a lay audience adopted the genre of commentary on the six non-naturals as the basis for organising his manual. In learned medicine the non-naturals were things external to the body whose effects could be modified through diet, drugs and regimen.[36] Accordingly chapter one is about air, chapter two is about meat and drink, chapter three is on sleeping and waking, chapter four considers exercise and rest, chapter five discusses evacuations and their obstructions, while chaper six deals with the passions, which Cheyne argues have "a greater influence on health and long life than most people are aware of". Although he does not dwell on them in detail here, Cheyne already identifies nervous diseases as those most associated with this influence.[37]

In conclusion to this chapter on the passions (to which we will later return) Cheyne observes that although medicine may help cure diseases that result from strong passions, "the *preventing* or *calming* the Passions themselves is the Business, not of Physick, but of *Virtue* and *Religion*".[38] This recognition of the limits to

---

35. Stanley W. Jackson, *Melancholia and Depression from Hippocratic Times to Modern Times*, New Haven 1986; Peter Melville Logan, *Nerves and Narratives: A Cultural History of Hysteria in Nineteenth-Century British Prose*, Berkeley, Los Angeles & London, 1997.
36. For an introduction to early modern theories of sickness and health, see Mary Lindemann, *Medicine and Society in Early Modern Europe*, Cambridge, 1999, pp. 8–36.
37. George Cheyne, *An Essay of Health*, p. 144.
38. ibid., p. 171.

medicine helps explain why Cheyne adds a seventh chapter to the more familiar six, entitled "Miscellany Observations", a maneuver which allows him to link the non-naturals to the seven deadly sins. In sum, Cheyne's *Essay* offers a compelling moral framework within which the patient is encouraged to practice self-management and to conduct his life responsibly, a way of life which demands simplicity, self-control and moderation in all things.[39]

A context for these moral injunctions is already found in the *Philosophical Principles of Natural Religion* (1705), an early work which Cheyne intended to be used as a means of instilling principles of natural religion into young men who were studying at Oxford or Cambridge. This title deliberately recalled Newton's *Philosophical Principles*, and was in fact written shortly after Newton became President of the Royal Society (1703), and Cheyne had joined his circle of admirers. In this work Cheyne uses Newton's laws of gravitational attraction both to refute Descartes's mechanistic theory of planetary and animal motion, and also to argue that the preservation of all bodies in rest or motion "depends on Almighty God as a cause". He also makes a direct analogy between the human spirit (the medium of musical spirit) and Newtonian gravity, each being active, motive principles bestowed direct on nature by God.[40]

The *Essay of Health* is also written in a style that deliberately recalls Newton's *Principia*. Cheyne structured the *Essay* as a series of Propositions and Scholia about the nature of bodies and their motions. From a series of initial axioms readers are to understand that the soul may be understood as a "homunculus" in the brain, that man is a compound of soul and body, and that this compound is inscribed in the Laws of Nature, which can only be

---

39. For earlier examples of physicians offering moral medicine see Andrew Cunningham, "Medicine to Calm the Mind: Boerhaave's Medical System, and Why It Was Adopted in Edinburgh", in: Andrew Cunningham and Roger French (eds.), *The Medical Enlightenment of the Eighteenth Century*, Cambridge 1990, pp. 40–66.
40. George Cheyne, *Philosophical Principles of Natural Religion; Containing the Elements of Natural Philosophy, and the Proofs for Natural Religion, Arising from Them*, London 1705, p. 13.

known through their effects, which is to say, experimentally. Here, as in the *Philosophical Principles*, Cheyne draws a direct comparison between the "infinitely fine and elastick fluid or Spirit" that Newton speculated might cause gravity, and the intermediate, material substance that "may make the cement between the human Soul and Body, and may be the Instrument or Medium of all its Actions and Functions" (i.e. the human spirit, or sensitive soul described by Willis). Just as there are principles of gravity or attraction inherent in bodies, so there may be an analogous principle of "Charity" in the animal spirits.[41]

Cheyne uses precisely the same analogy in the first section of *The English Malady*, which is a philosophical introduction to the nature and causes of nervous diseases. However, readers are advised to skip this section if they just want to learn about successful cures and treatments that are found in the second and third parts of the book. Instead of reading the first part in detail, all readers are asked to do is imagine that the human body is "a machine of an infinite number of and variety of different channels and pipes, filled with various and different liquors and fluids, perpetually running ... and sending out little branches and outlets, to moisten, nourish, and repair the expenses of living." They also have to suppose that the intelligent principle, or soul, is situated somewhere in the brain, where the nerves, or "instruments of sensation" terminate. The soul is to be imagined as a musician, while the nerves are like keys of an organ which, on being touched, convey the sound and harmony to the musician, who is in a well-framed and well-tuned organ case.[42]

Perhaps assuming that this organ model is still too complex for most readers to comprehend, Cheyne goes on to offer a "more gross similitude" where the soul is now imagined as a bell in a steeple, one with an infinite number of clappers. Attached to these clappers are the nerves, ropes which are distributed to all extremeties of the body. On being touched or pulled, each nerve conveys an impulse or stroke that immediately makes the bell

---

41. Cheyne, *An Essay of Health*, p. 146.
42. Cheyne, *English Malady*, pp. 4–5.

sound.[43] At this point Cheyne finally admits all these ways of thinking about how the mind and body influence each other are inadequate, and hopes that those acquainted with "the best philosophy" will go on to read what he has to say in the rest of this section, which also includes another discussion of the Newtonian ether, and its relevance to health.

The ether is relevant to Cheyne's theory of health chiefly because the nerves are to be thought of as "bundles of solid, springy, and elastic Threads or Filaments" that depend on the action of spirits (equivalent to the ether) for their responsiveness. In their optimum, well-tempered state, these threads are highly elastic or springy, and responsive to the intentions of the mind, and as a result make good music. The healthy body in short, is like a musical instrument that properly responds to the touch of the player:

> Since the *mind* resides, as has been said, in the common *sensory*, like a skilful Musician by a *well-tuned Instrument*; if the *Organ* be found, duly tempered and exactly adjusted ... the *Musick* will be *distinct, agreeable* and *harmonious*. But if the *Organ* be spoiled and broken ... it will not answer the Intention of the *Musician*, nor yield any distinctive Sound, or true *Harmony*.[44]

From this analogy it is a comparatively short step to construct a physiology of the nervous system (based on no discernable evidence whatever) that mirrors different psychological states. Thus people with the "most *springy, lively* and *elastick* Fibres have the quickest sensations", and because of this they generally excel in the faculty of imagination, which (as we have seen from Willis's work) was thought to be located in one of the ventricles of the brain. Yet it is precisely these intelligent, sensitive, and imaginative people — notably those who lead "sedentary Lives, or indulge in contemplative Studies" — who are most likely to be affected by nervous diseases, disorders that are caused by the nerves becoming weakened through excessive stimulation. Sensitivity, in other words, is

---

43. Both these models recall René Descartes's description of the "animal machine" from his *De homine figuris* (completed c. 1633 and published 1662); see Kassler, *Inner Music*, pp. 43–48.
44. Cheyne, *An Essay of Health*, p. 158.

both valuable and dangerous, in that it may lead to enervation and ill health as much as delight.

By contrast, people who have inelastic organs of sensation that do not respond quickly to mental or physical impulses enjoy much better health than their more sensitive counterparts. The misfortune of those who do not suffer from strong passions, however, is that they are unfeeling. As Cheyne contemptuously puts it, "such are *Ideots*, *Peasants* and *Mechanicks*, and all those we call Indolent people". This putatively medical, but also clearly moral, distinction between the refined and vulgar pandered to the sensibilities of the upwardly mobile middle classes, whose members wanted to distinguish themselves from their inferiors. And while cultivated men were certainly diagnosed with the "English disease" it was notably women who looked to Cheyne for treatment of, and explanation for, their nervous complaints.[45]

Given the emphasis that Cheyne places on the body as a sympathetic and well-tuned musical instrument, it comes as something of a surprise to discover that music's power over the mind and body actually finds no place in his reflections on health and nervous disease. This neglect is all the more striking when we consider that music's ability to raise and quell the passions was a fashionable topic in the elite circles within which Cheyne moved. Indeed, he was practising medicine during a period when "for the first time in Western history music claims its rightful place in the world of culture … becoming a topic of discussion in aristocratic salons and in learned salons of all kinds".[46]

MUSIC AND MORALITY

As I suggested at the beginning of this paper, and have gone on to argue in more detail with reference to three specific individuals, to talk learnedly (i.e. "philosophically") about music and its effects

---

45. See Guerrini, *Obesity and Depression*. On earlier manifestations of this connection, see Juliana Schiesari, *The Gendering of Melancholia: Feminism, Psychoanalysis, and the Symbolics of Loss in Renaissance Literature*, Ithaca and London 1992.
46. Enrico Fubini (ed.), *Music and Culture in Eighteenth-Century Europe: A Source Book*, Chicago and London, 1994, p. 1.

was certainly acceptable within the British social elite during our chosen period (1650–1750). However, it by no means followed that the ability to *perform* music well indicated high intellectual, or even social, status, especially in a society where the monarch himself (as with William of Orange, for example) regarded music as an expensive feminine luxury, and the professional musical scene was increasingly dominated by foreign talent.[47] In late seventeenth- and early eighteenth-century Britain, a learned physician or mathematician was certainly not expected to play skillfully, even though he might be a knowledgable patron and amateur — as for example Viscount William Brouncker (c. 1620–1684), the Royal Society of London's first President, or Dr John Gregory (1724–1773), another Scottish physician who became a Fellow of the Society in 1754.

Indeed, the indifference that Britain's greatest natural philosopher apparently showed towards music only seems to emphasize his intellectual stature, rather than any lack of imagination. Posterity records that Newton went to a single opera in his lifetime, which he left before the third act, and on the occasion of hearing Handel play upon the harpsichord found, "nothing worthy to remark but the elasticity of his fingers".[48] These apocryphal tales can perhaps also help illuminate why Cheyne does not discuss music in his treatment of nervous disease, even while agreeing with Newton that the universe is fundamentally "musical" in nature.[49]

For both Newton and Cheyne, I believe, the problem with actual music was precisely because it can stir the passions so

---

47. Reflected, for example, in King William's decision to drastically cut expenditure on his private musicians (including Purcell) in 1690 while maintaining his military bands; see Peter Holman, *Four and Twenty Fiddlers: The Violin at the English Court 1540–1690*, Oxford 1993.
48. The account of Newton's visit to the opera comes from the Rev. William Stukeley, *Diary*, 18 April 1720, while the story about Handel's fingers has been attributed both to John Hawkins, *Life of Samuel Johnson*, London 1787, and also to Joseph Warton, *Works of Alexander Pope*, London 1797. I can find no trace of it in either work through a word search in *Eighteenth Century Collections Online* (Thompson Gale Publications).
49. In contrast to Cheyne's neglect of music, there is an entire chapter on "The powers of music in soothing the passions, and allaying the Tempests of the Soul" in Nicholas Robinson's *New System of the Spleen, Vapours, and Hypochondriack Melancholy*, London 1729, pp. 343–49.

deeply, having an effect on the soul which philosophers since Plato have regarded with ambivalence. As the *Republic* makes clear, all is well with individuals and the state so long as musicians adhere to the natural laws of harmony, and the goal of philosophy is to pursue the highest good. However, if fundamental, God-given laws are transgressed, and music is left unregulated, corruption and sickness will inevitably follow — and there was no shortage of critics who thought modern, commercial music was a corrupting influence in early eighteenth-century London society.[50]

Considered in this light, Newton's impatience with Italian opera may have been due to its apparent neglect of harmonic principles (at least in his judgement), all the while pandering to vulgar taste. A similar distaste for modern, corrupt practice and desire to recreate the purity of ancient music (in tandem with the recovery of ancient philosophy) seems to have underpinned Newton's endorsement of Salmon's attempts during the late 1680s to design lutes and other fretted instruments that could be played using the pure consonances of just intonation (harmonic ratios which Kepler had earlier found to be immanent in the motion of the planets) rather than the impure intervals of equal temperament. For despite his support for Salmon's musical experiments, it is clear that the only harmony Newton cared about was silent, abstract structure, not the sensual impact of lived musical experience.[51]

A similar ambiguity is implicit in Cheyne's "musical" model of the body as the instrument of the soul. As I have demonstrated, although his explanation of health and disease is couched in secular, medical terms, the message to patients is nevertheless deeply moral in nature, offering guidance and comfort to those suffering from the excesses of civilized life. Also, Cheyne's model of health is based on a concept of harmony, or balance, rather than on musical sound itself, this being understood as an external stimulus that has an immediate effect on the auditory nerves and animal spirits. Granted, this model allows that the "well-tuned" nervous system will respond sympathetically to good music, and that an early

---

50. See William Weber, *The Rise of Musical Classics in Eighteenth-Century England*, Oxford 1992.
51. Gouk, *Music, Science and Natural Magic*, pp. 230–2, 257.

training in music may have the effect of refining the nerves and improving mental functioning, a suggestion already made by Willis in the 1670s and developed later by Enlightenment physicians such as John Gregory in his *Comparative view of the State and Faculties of Man* (1763).[52]

However, Cheyne's doctrine of the nerves also suggests that the *wrong kind* of music (however defined) — or simply *too much* music — can be bad for people, especially if indulged in to excess. This conclusion may seem to have moved us some distance from our academy's topic of Baroque music theory, but in reality it may bring us closer to its heart, a theme which from Kircher to Diderot was music's power to move the human passions — a force for good when properly applied, but one which could also have damaging effects both on the individual and on society as a whole.

---

52. See Penelope Gouk, "Music's Pathological and Therapeutic Effects on the Body Politic: Doctor John Gregory's Views" in Penelope Gouk and Helen Hills (eds.) Representing Emotions: New Connections in the Histories of Art, Music and Medicine, Aldershot 2005, pp. 191–207.

L'ÉDITION DE LA POLYPHONIE FRANÇAISE DU 17ᵉ SIÈCLE

Gérard Geay

Éditer la musique ancienne nécessite une profonde connaissance du contexte théorique et pratique dans lequel les œuvres ont vu le jour. Par exemple, il est indispensable de maîtriser le système modal, la solmisation et les règles du contrepoint pour pouvoir juger si le texte musical de la source est correct et, dans le cas contraire, être capable de le corriger en respectant le style de l'époque.

L'Atelier d'étude et les Éditions du Centre de Musique Baroque de Versailles publient depuis plusieurs années des polyphonies profanes ou religieuses françaises. Tous ces compositeurs forment le chaînon manquant entre ce qu'il est convenu d'appeler schématiquement la Renaissance et le Grand Siècle de Louis XIV. Cependant, ils ne constituent pas un groupe homogène. En effet, nous pouvons distinguer plusieurs générations:

– Eustache Du Caurroy, né en 1549;
– Nicolas Formé, né en 1567;
– Pierre Guédron, né dans les années 1570;
– Antoine Boësset, Guillaume Bouzignac, peut-être Jean Boyer, nés dans les années 1580;
– Henri Frémart, mort en 1651 et maître des enfants de chœur à la cathédrale de Rouen dès 1611;
– Étienne Moulinié, né vers 1600;
– Jean-Baptiste Boësset, né en 1614;
– Pierre Menault, né en 1642.

Nous devons donc déterminer dans quelle mesure le style évolue durant toute cette période. Pour tenter d'établir une chronologie, nous pouvons aussi prendre en compte la date des sources en les complétant avec quelques sources d'œuvres instrumentales qui jouent un rôle important dans notre recherche, sans oublier que la date de publication ne correspond pas toujours avec la date de composition[1] :

---
1. Voyez la bibliographie à la fin de cet article.

– 1602 :	Livre 0 des airs de Pierre Guédron[2] (Veuve Ballard et Pierre Ballard);
– 1608 :	Livre I des airs de Pierre Guédron (Pierre Ballard);
– 1609 :	les Preces ecclesiasticæ d'Eustache Du Caurroy (Pierre Ballard);
– 1610 :	les Fantasies d'Eustache Du Caurroy (Pierre Ballard);
– 1613 :	Livre II des airs de Pierre Guédron (Pierre Ballard);
– 1617/1618 :	Livre III des airs de Pierre Guédron (Pierre Ballard);
– 1618 :	Livre IV des airs de Pierre Guédron (Pierre Ballard);
– 1619 :	les Airs à quatre parties de Jean Boyer (Pierre Ballard);
– 1620 :	Livre V des airs de Pierre Guédron (Pierre Ballard);
– 1620/1638 ? :	le Cantique de la Vierge Marie de Nicolas Formé (F-Pn/ ms 1870);
– 1623 :	les Hymnes de l'Eglise de Jehan Titelouze (Pierre Ballard?);
– 1624 :	la deuxième édition des Hymnes de l'Eglise de Jehan Titelouze (Pierre Ballard);
– 1626 :	le Magnificat de Jehan Titelouze (Pierre Ballard);
– 1638 :	la Musica simplex de Nicolas Formé (Pierre Ballard); la Missa duobus Choris et les motets Ecce tu pulchra es, Domine salvum fac regem de Nicolas Formé (Pierre Ballard);
– 1642/1645 :	les huit messes de Henri Frémart (Robert III Ballard);
– 1650 ? :	les motets et les chansons de Guillaume Bouzignac (Recueil de motets et chansons de Tours F-TO/ ms 108);
– 1650/1660 ? :	les motets, les chansons et la Messe à sept parties de Guillaume Bouzignac (Recueil Deslauriers F-Pn/ Rés Vma ms 571);
– 1663 :	la Missa Macula non est in te de Louis Le Prince (Robert III Ballard);
– 1665 :	Livre d'orgue... de Guillaume-Gabriel Nivers (Robert III Ballard);
– 1667 :	2. Livre d'orgue... de Guillaume-Gabriel Nivers (Robert III Ballard);

---

2. Dans cette chronologie succincte, nous ne tenons pas compte de la publication des airs de Guédron avec tablature de luth.

L'Édition de la polyphonie française du 17ᵉ siècle

- 1668 : Meslanges de sujets chrestiens d'Étienne Moulinié (Jacques de Senlecque);
- 1675 : 3. Livre d'orgue des huit tons de l'Eglise de Guillaume-Gabriel Nivers (Robert III Ballard);
- 1687 : la Missa Ave senior Stephane de Pierre Menault (Christophe Ballard);
- 1691 : la Missa Ferte rosas de Pierre Menault (Christophe Ballard);
- 1692 : la Missa Date lilia de Pierre Menault (Christophe Ballard).

Les résultats de l'analyse de ces partitions doivent être comparés avec les traités de composition contemporains. Vous en trouverez la liste dans la bibliographie.

L'ORDRE DES MODES

Le système modal en usage en France au début du XVIIᵉ siècle est directement issu des développements qu'a connus le XVIᵉ siècle. En 1547, Glarean explique, dans son Dodecachordon, qu'il n'y a pas seulement huit tons (un authente et un plagal sur D, E, F et G) mais bien douze. Pour obtenir ce résultat, il place une octave sur chacun des sept degrés de l'échelle musicale : A, B, C, D, E, F et G, et la divise soit arithmétiquement (par la quarte, chiffrée 4), ce qui donne un ton plagal, soit harmoniquement (par la quinte, chiffrée 5), ce qui donne un ton authente. Dans notre tableau, les finales sont imprimées en caractères gras et la numérotation des tons figure au-dessous :

Intervalles	A / **D** / A	A / E / **A**	B / **E** / B	B / F / **B**	C / **F** / C	C / G / **C**	D / **G** / D	D / A / **D**	E / **A** / E	E / B / **E**	F / **B** / F	F / C / **F**	G / **C** / G	G / D / **G**
Divisions	4	5	4	5	4	5	4	5	4	+4	5	4	5	
Tons	2ᵉ	9ᵉ	4ᵉ	✗	6ᵉ	11ᵉ	8ᵉ	1ᵉʳ	10ᵉ	3ᵉ	✗	5ᵉ	12ᵉ	7ᵉ

Certes, sept degrés divisés deux fois donnent quatorze intervalles. Mais la division harmonique de l'octave B-F-B et la division arithmétique de l'octave F-B-F donnent respectivement la quinte diminuée B-F et la quarte augmentée F-B, intervalles qui ne

Gérard Geay

permettent pas de construire un ton sur la finale B. Nous obtenons donc bien six tons plagaux et six authentes sur A, C, D, E, F et G, soit en tout douze tons ou modes. (Ce n'est pas l'objet de cet article d'aborder la question de la terminologie, les mots ton et mode étant ici synonymes.)

Dans la première édition de 1558 des Istitutioni Harmoniche (p. 309 et suivantes), Zarlino reprend la proposition de Glarean. Mais dans ses Dimostrationi harmoniche de 1571 (p. 270 et suivantes), il dispose les douze tons selon l'ordre des syllabes de l'hexacorde guidonien: *ut, re, mi, fa, sol* et *la*, disposition qu'il adoptera dans l'édition de 1573 des Istitutioni Harmoniche (p. 366 et suivantes). En 1639, Antoine Parran, dans son Traité de la mvsique (p. 112–135), fait la distinction entre les *huict Modes, ou Tons de l'Eglise*, les *douze Modes anciens*, dont la disposition correspond à celle de l'édition de 1558 des Istitutioni Harmoniche, et les *douze Modes des modernes*. Ce que nous pouvons visualiser grâce au tableau suivant:

	Modes ecclésiastiques	Modes anciens	Modes des modernes	Dénomination hellénisante
1er	**D-A-D**	**D-A-D**	C-G-C	Dorique
2e	A-**D**-A	A-**D**-A	G-**C**-G	Sousdorique
3e	**E-B-E**	**E-B-E**	**D-A-D**	Phrygien
4e	B-**E**-B	B-**E**-B	A-**D**-A	Sousphrygien
5e	**F-C-F**	**F-C-F**	**E-B-E**	Lydien
6e	C-**F**-C	C-**F**-C	B-**E**-B	Souslydien
7e	**G-D-G**	**G-D-G**	**F-C-F**	Mixolydien
8e	D-**G**-D	D-**G**-D	C-**F**-C	Sousmixolydien
9e		**A-E-A**	**G-D-G**	Æolien
10e		E-**A**-E	D-**G**-D	Sousæolien
11e		**C-G-C**	**A-E-A**	Ionien ou Iastien
12e		G-**C**-G	E-**A**-E	Sousionien ou sousiastien

Remarquons que si la numérotation des modes anciens et des modes des modernes change, le 1er mode authente ancien sur D devenant le 3e mode des modernes, leur dénomination hellénisante ne change pas, ce qui n'est pas sans nous surprendre puisque, dans les textes théoriques, l'éthos des modes se rapporte à la dénomination. (Nous ne traiterons pas en détail de l'éthos des modes qui n'est pas le sujet principal de cet article.) Le 1er mode des modernes sur C se retrouvera exprimer à peu près les mêmes passions que le 1ᵉʳ mode ancien sur D, tout deux étant dénommé Dorique (Parran, p. 117 à 119) :

Premier mode des anciens sur D

Le premier Authentique & plus graue c'est le Dorique, propre pour le chant pieux, il est severe, belliqueux, meslé de grauité, & d'allegresse.

Premier mode des modernes sur C

Le premier Mode Dorique, belliqueux, pieux, & propre à l'entretien de prudence, c'est l'vt de C fa vt.

En tant qu'*vnziesme mode des anciens*, le mode sur C est qualifié de :

> *Ionien ou Ionique, selon l'opinion de Porphyrion, appelé aussi Iastien par Aristoxene, il est jouial, & propre pour les recreations & dances, & se commence en C sol vt fa.*

Alors que l'ancien Dorien sur D devient, comme *troisiesme mode des modernes* :

> *le Phrygien, propre pour exciter à cholere.*

Parran (p. 121) relève cette incohérence en avouant modestement son ignorance de la vraie nature des modes grecs :

> *Vous noterez aussi, qu'encores que j'aye dit cy dessus auec plusieurs autres que le premier Mode, qui commence par vt, c'est le Dorique : toutefois il est vray semblable que c'est l'Ionique, ou Iastien* [3], *& que ré c'est le Dorique, &c. La raison & la probabilité que j'ay eu de mettre la Dorique en l'vt de C fa vt, & ainsi des autres, a esté que nous ne sçauons point asseurément quelle estoit la Dorique & Ionique des Anciens (c'est à dire des Grecs), &c. & partant je laisse la chose libre & indifferente.*

LA STRUCTURE DES MODES

A l'exception de l'analyse des huit messes de Frémart, notre recherche porte actuellement plutôt sur les modes mineurs dont les différences sont plus marquées que celles entre les modes

---

3. Parran veut dire par là que c'est le 11ᵉ mode ancien qui commence par ut et non pas le Dorien.

majeurs. Nous nous limiterons donc ici à une simple comparaison entre leurs structures au moyen des deux tableaux suivants :

Les trois modes mineurs sur D, E et A
(les demi-tons sont indiqués par les grisés) :

I	II	III	IV	V	VI	VII	I
D	E	F	G	A	B	C	D
E	F	G	A	B	C	D	E
A	B	C	D	E	F	G	A

Le mode sur E se distingue des deux autres par sa tierce mineure E-G où le demi-ton se trouve entre I et II, alors que, dans les deux autres modes, il se trouve entre II et III. Le mode sur D se distingue par sa 6te majeure entre D et B, le demi-ton supérieur se plaçant par conséquent entre VI et VII, alors que, dans les deux autres modes, il se trouve entre V-VI. Enfin, si les trois modes ont une 7e mineure, la 6te F-D, sur II, est majeure dans le mode sur E, alors que E-C et B-G sont mineures dans les deux autres modes. Cette 6te mineure devra donc être altérée pour aller à l'8^{ve} dans les cadences. Nous allons y revenir.

Les trois modes majeurs sur F, G et C
(les demi-tons sont indiqués par les grisés) :

I	II	III	IV	V	VI	VII	I
F	G	A	B	C	D	E	F
G	A	B	C	D	E	F	G
C	D	E	F	G	A	B	C

Le mode sur F se distingue par la présence du triton F-B entre I et IV, alors que les deux autres modes ont une 4te juste. Dans la pratique, ce B est souvent bémolisé afin de chanter une 4te juste avec la finale F. Le mode sur G se distingue par sa 7e mineure qui fait que la 6te sur II, A-F, y est mineure, alors qu'elle est majeure dans les deux autres modes. Cette 6te mineure devra donc être altérée pour aller à l'8^{ve} dans les cadences. Nous comprenons que l'emploi du B♭ sur le IV de F et du F# sur le VII de G aboutit à la fusion de deux échelles et de celle sur C en un seul et unique mode majeur et que le mode sur C s'est progressivement imposé comme archétype étant le seul des trois constitué uniquement de degrés naturels :

Les trois modes majeurs sur F, G et C avec leur altération
(les demi-tons sont indiqués par les grisés) :

I	II	III	IV	V	VI	VII	I
F	G	A	B♭	C	D	E	F
G	A	B	C	D	E	F#	G
C	D	E	F	G	A	B	C

Grâce aux altérations, les trois modes ont leur demi-ton entre III-IV et VII-I. Mais, dans la musique modale du XVIIe siècle français, cette identité structurelle n'est qu'apparente. En effet, un degré altéré est, d'un point de vue conceptuel, fondamentalement différent du même degré naturel et la possibilité même de l'altérer ou non participe de la caractérisation du mode.

Pour terminer, précisons que les huit tons ecclésiastiques se transposent. La transposition la plus courante se fait par bémol (nous verrons le sens exact de cette expression dans le paragraphe consacré à la solmisation), selon le schéma suivant :

	Tons naturels	Tons transposés
Armure	rien	un B♭
Protus	sur D	sur G
Deuterus	sur E	sur A
Tritus	sur F	sur B♭
Tetrardus	sur G	sur C

Sauf le cas particulier du Tritus, la présence d'un bémol à l'armure indique donc généralement que la pièce est composée dans un mode transposé, le plus courant au XVIIe siècle étant de loin le Dorien sur G, ancêtre du G mineur classique.

Il est temps maintenant d'introduire une notion bien connue dans le domaine de la monodie modale mais peu utilisée dans l'analyse de la polyphonie : le degré mobile.

Gérard Geay

LE DEGRÉ MOBILE

L'origine du degré mobile remonte aux huit tons ecclésiastiques. Il s'agissait alors de doter le premier tétracorde du tritus, F-B, d'un demi-ton, à l'image des trois autres tétracordes :

Tétracordes						
Protus	D	E	F	G		
Deuterus		E	F	G	A	
Tritus			F	G	A	b
Tetrardus				G	A	♮	C

Certes, la structure intervallique du tétracorde du Tritus et celle du Tetrardus (ton, ton, demi-ton) est identique. Mais pour un chanteur du Moyen âge, comme d'ailleurs pour un chanteur du XVIIe siècle, ce n'était pas la même chose de chanter par bémol (b) et de chanter par bécarre (♮). De plus, le IVe degré du tritus est mobile, celui de tetrardus ne l'est pas, l'emploi d'un C# étant totalement exclu.

Tritus	F	G	A	b	♮	C	D	E	F
Tetrardus	G	A	B	C		D	E	F	G

Ce b mol est particulièrement employé dans les tons où la 4te F-B se rencontre souvent : en Protus authente (1er ton sur D), en Deuterus plagal (4e ton sur E) en Tritus (5e et 6e tons sur F) et même en Tetrardus (sur G) bien que la minorisation de la tierce du mode fût souvent critiquée parce qu'elle transformait ce mode en Protus transposé. A ce propos, voici un exemple de *fa super la* dans l'hexacorde par nature en Tetrardus dans le 4e verset du Magnificat du septiesme mode de Formé (mes. 15, au Contra) :

(voir page suivante)

Vous en trouverez deux autres exemples mes. 24 au Bassus et mes. 65 au Contra. Par contre, le bémol proposé par l'éditeur, mes. 8 au Tenor, est peu probable, cette voix étant en hexacorde par ♮ carre. (Pour les notions de *fa super la* et d'hexacorde, veuillez vous reporter au paragraphe suivant.)

L'Édition de la polyphonie française du 17e siècle

Nicolas Formé. *Œuvres complètes, p. 39, mes. 12-15*

Ce même degré mobile se retrouve dans la polyphonie où il s'agit soit de chanter la 4te juste sur ♮ soit de chanter la 5te juste sur B. Ce que nous pouvons résumer par cette règle : dans un intervalle parfait, il ne faut pas chanter *mi contra fa*. D'où la nécessité d'aborder maintenant la question de la solmisation.

LA SOLMISATION

Nous nous limiterons ici aux généralités nécessaires à la compréhension de notre propos. Guido d'Arezzo développe sa méthode au début du XIe siècle. C'est un moyen mnémotechnique pour apprendre les intervalles et repérer la place du demi-ton. Beaucoup d'étudiants se demandent pourquoi Guido utilisait un hexacorde alors que les modes s'inscrivent dans une 8^{ve}. Une réponse qui, aujourd'hui encore, nous semble satisfaisante serait que l'hexacorde englobe les trois tétracordes, comme le schéma suivant le montre :

bécarre	Γ	A	♮	C	D	E
nature	C	D	E	F	G	a
bémol	F	G	A	b	C	D
1er tétracorde :	*ut*	*re*	*mi*	*fa*		
2e tétracorde :		*re*	*mi*	*fa*	*sol*	
3e tétracorde :			*mi*	*fa*	*sol*	*la*
Hexacorde :	*ut*	*re*	*mi*	*fa*	*sol*	*la*
	3^{ce} majeure			3^{ce} majeure		

La lettre grecque Γ fut choisie pour différencier le premier degré de l'échelle musicale de G, g et gg lorsqu'il fut ajouté sous l'ancien premier degré A. Les auteurs anciens y voient généralement l'origine étymologique du mot gamme. L'hexacorde est constitué de deux tierces majeures séparées par un demi-ton. L'avantage de cette méthode parfaitement adaptée à la musique ancienne réside dans le fait que tout demi-ton se solmisera *mi-fa*. Il ne reste donc plus qu'à pratiquer la *deductio*, c'est à dire à placer les syllabes sur l'échelle musicale sachant qu'il y a trois sortes de demi-ton pour reconstituer l'ensemble du système :

1) par bécarre entre le ♮ quadratum ou durum et le C ;
2) par nature entre le E et le F ;
3) par bémol entre le A et le b rotundum ou mollum.

Les hexacordes prennent le nom de leur demi-ton soit, dans l'ordre d'apparition du grave à l'aigu :

1) par bécarre entre Γ et E ;
2) par nature entre C et A ;
3) par bémol entre F et d ;

et ainsi de suite :

	bécarre	nature	bémol	bécarre	nature	bémol	bécarre
ee							la
dd						la	sol
cc					sol	fa	
♮♮							mi
bb						fa	
aa					la	mi	re
g					sol	re	ut
f					fa	ut	
e				la	mi		
d			la	sol	re		
c			sol	fa	ut		
♮				mi			
b			fa				
a		la	mi	re			
G		sol	re	ut			
F		fa	ut				
E	la	mi					
D	sol	re					
C	fa	ut					
♮	mi						
A	re						
Γ	ut						

Au XVIIe siècle, la solmisation est toujours pratiquée, mais sous une forme simplifiée comme l'explique Parran (p. 12, chapitre VI.

L'Édition de la polyphonie française du 17ᵉ siècle

Methode facile pour apprendre la Musique:

> *La Game ancienne a eu autre-fois sa vogue, comme estant tres-bonne, & vtile: voire necessaire à ceux qui apprennent a composer: mais de trop longue haleine: en ce temps icy, comme les esprits s'aiguisent, & subtilisent tous les jours, on a trouué vn chemin plus court, qui aide, & soulage fort la memoire. C'est vne main ou alphabet de Musique recent, & plein d'artifice: pour ce qu'on y trouve, par ordre vt, ré, mi, fa, sol, la par b mol, Nature, & ♮ dur, comme il s'ensuit.*

Par [b] mol. Par Nature. Par ♮ Dur

E		mi	la
D	la	re	sol
C	sol	vt	fa
B	fa	♮	mi
A	mi	la	re
G	re	sol	vt
F	vt	fa	

Ce texte est particulièrement intéressant parce qu'il explique que la *Game ancienne* était *necessaire à ceux qui apprennent a composer*. La solmisation était donc bien plus qu'un simple solfège pour débutants comme certains ont tendance à le croire aujourd'hui. Elle était certainement l'un des fondements du système musical aux côtés de la modalité et du contrepoint et, de ce fait, constitue un paramètre indispensable à prendre en compte de nos jours dans l'analyse des œuvres.

Outre les traités, nous trouvons dans les sources musicales elles-mêmes de nombreuses preuves de la pratique encore vivante de la solmisation au XVIIᵉ siècle. Voyez, par exemple, dans Frémart et Guédron. Elles sont essentiellement de deux ordres :

1) l'absence du bémol dans les cas où la note ne peut pas être naturelle: saut mélodique de 4ᵗᵉ obligatoirement juste; 5ᵗᵉ entre deux parties obligatoirement juste;
2) présence d'un bécarre ou d'un dièse de précaution là où le chanteur aurait pu choisir de chanter un bémol.

L'altération de précaution est essentiellement utilisée dans le cas du *fa super hexacordum* ou *fa super la*. Lorsque la mélodie excède l'hexacorde d'un seul degré, ce septième degré se chante *fa* sans autre muance. Bien qu'il s'agisse d'un demi-ton, le degré inférieur se chante non pas *mi* mais *la*, alors qu'au contraire la muance fait apparaître le nouveau demi-ton chanté *mi-fa*. La muance ou *mutatio* consiste à changer de syllabe pour passer d'un hexacorde à un autre. Par exemple, dans notre schéma à la dernière syllabe *la*, qui ne peut que descendre dans l'hexacorde par nature, est substituée la syllabe *re* qui permet de monter dans l'hexacorde par ♮ carre. Ce n'est pas le lieu ici de détailler ce procédé :

Exemples de *fa super la* et de muance de nature à ♮ carre

Hexacorde par nature avec *fa super la*							
ut	re	mi	fa	sol	la	fa	la
C	D	E	F	G	A	B	A
Hexacorde par b mol avec *fa super la*							
ut	re	mi	fa	sol	la	fa	la
F	G	a	b	c	d	e	d
Hexacorde par nature					Hexacorde par ♮ carre		
ut	re	mi	fa	sol	re	mi	fa
C	D	E	F	G	A	B	C

Pour éviter que le chanteur bémolise spontanément ce degré, le copiste ou l'imprimeur utilisera un ♮ de précaution signifiant : chantez *mi* et non pas *fa*, c'est à dire un ton et non pas un demi-ton au-dessus.

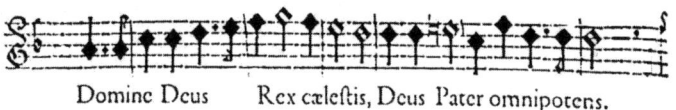

Domine Deus   Rex cæleſtis, Deus Pater omnipotens.

Cantus de la Missa Paratum cor meum Deus
(Henri Frémart. Œuvres complètes, p. XCIX)
© Clichés Guildhall Library, London (Gresham Music Collection)

Cet exemple est particulièrement intéressant parce que le ♮ de précaution sur *Pater* pourrait sembler superflu considérant que les trois mesures précédentes sont dans l'hexacorde par nature dans lequel E se chante *mi*. Peut-être a-t-on craint que les chanteurs muent sur le D de *Deus*, chanté alors *la* dans l'hexacorde par bémol au lieu de *re* dans celui par nature ?

L'Édition de la polyphonie française du 17ᵉ siècle

LA MUSICA FICTA

Tout ce qui a été exposé jusqu'ici concerne ce qu'on appelait la *musica recta*, c'est à dire l'emploi des degrés naturels des modes, le degré mobile en faisant partie. Or, dès le XIIIᵉ siècle, l'emploi d'autres altérations se développe, par exemple, dans les motets des derniers fascicules du manuscrit H 196 de la Faculté de médecine de Montpellier. C'est la *musica ficta* ou *finta* qui utilise d'autres degrés altérés. A notre connaissance, le plus ancien texte théorique traitant de cette question est le Compendium de discantu mensurabili de Petrus dictus palma ociosa datant de 1336 publié par Johannes Wolf au début du XXᵉ siècle. Ce texte est particulièrement intéressant pour nous parce qu'il aborde la *musica ficta* du point de vue du contrepoint. En résumé, l'auteur y explique que les intervalles imparfaits, la 3ᶜᵉ et la 6ᵗᵉ, doivent être le plus près possible de l'intervalle parfait, unisson, 5ᵗᵉ ou 8ᵛᵉ, auquel ils s'enchaînent, ce qui implique la présence d'un demi-ton dans l'une des deux parties, si besoin en utilisant le bémol ou le dièse. Même si le style a profondément changé depuis le XIVᵉ siècle, nous trouvons un écho très fort de ce principe médiéval dans la théorie française du XVIIᵉ siècle (Parran, p. 51, § 6) :

> *La Tierce, & la Sixiesme deuant l'Octaue, doiuent estre majeure, comme estant plus proches de leur terme : & la Tierce mineure deuant la Quinte, pour esuiter la fausse relation du Triton.*

Certes, Parran rejette la 3ᶜᵉ majeure devant la quinte, si courante au XIVᵉ siècle, pour cause de fausse relation, mais la pratique de son temps ne lui donne pas toujours raison car nous en trouvons chez Guédron, une trentaine d'années auparavant :

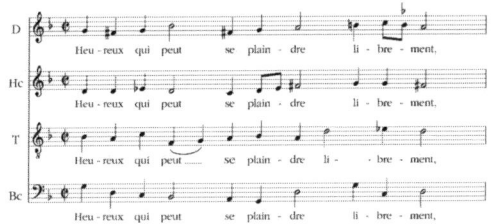

Air n° 77 *Heureux qui se peut plaindre* du Livre I de 1608

et chez Formé, entre 1620 et 1638 (dans le Magnificat du sixiesme mode, p. 34, mes. 20, et le Magnificat du septiesme mode, p. 43, mes. 66-67), alors que Frémart, dans les années 1640, ne l'emploie pas. Prenons deux autres citations qui confirment la pérennité de ces règles (Parran, p. 52, § 3) :

> *On va d'ordinaire de la Tierce mineure a l'Vnisson par mouuement contraire, & degrez conjoints...*

Antoine Parran, exemple C p. 54. Traité de mvsique... Minkoff, Genève, 1972

C'est exactement la règle médiévale. Par contre, la règle suivante mérite quelques éclaircissements (Parran, p. 52, § 5) :

> *Quand les deux parties montent ou descendent ensemble par degrez conjoints ou separez en vne partie, ou en toutes les deux, allant de la Tierce a la Quinte, cela se peut faire par la Tierce majeure, ou mineure: toutefois quelques vns estiment la majeure meilleure.*

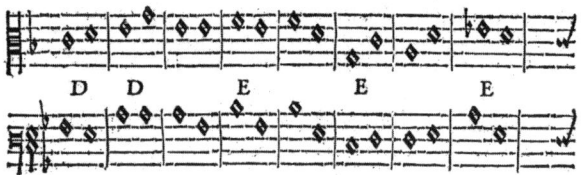

Antoine Parran, exemple E p. 54. Traité de mvsique... Minkoff, Genève, 1972

Il ressort de l'examen des exemples que Parran mélange en fait deux règles concernant l'enchaînement de la 3ce à la 5te en descendant et en montant. En descendant, les trois exemples musicaux comportent bien, comme au Moyen âge, une 3ce mineure, la troisième étant d'ailleurs bémolisée. Cependant, l'analyse musicale montre que la tierce n'était pas toujours mineure dans ce cas dans les œuvres du XVIIe siècle. La fin de la règle: *cela se peut faire par la Tierce majeure, ou mineure: toutefois quelques vns estiment la majeure meilleure*, ne concerne que l'enchaînement en montant dont les deux exemples comportent respectivement la 3ce mineure et la 3ce majeure. Ces règles expliquent la présence dans la polyphonie française du XVIIe siècle d'altérations qui « altèrent » l'échelle du mode. Ce sont, à proprement parler, des degrés mobiles qui peuvent obéir aussi bien aux règles d'enchaînement des intervalles contrapunctiques qu'aux règles de la solmisation.

Le tableau suivant montre en grisés quels sont les degrés des trois modes mineurs qui sont susceptibles de porter des intervalles altérés. Ce sont principalement les 3ces et les 6tes qui sont concernées, les intervalles mineurs pouvant être majorisés et les majeurs minorisés :

I	II		III		IV		V	VI		VII	
A	B		C	C#	D		E	F	F#	G	G#
D		E	F	F#	G	G#	A	B♭	B	C	C#
E	F	F#	G	G#	A		B	C	C#	D	

- 2de majeure
- 3ce majeure
- triton
- 6te mineure
- 6te majeure
- 7e majeure

Nous touchons là à une différence essentielle entre l'ancienne polyphonie et le système tonal. Dans ce dernier, les accords portés par chaque degré du mode majeur et du mode mineur sont identiques dans les douze tons. C'est le principe même de l'enseignement de l'accompagnement et de la composition *selon la règle des octaves de musique* tel que l'expose Campion dans son Traité de 1716. Alors que dans les modes, ils sont susceptibles d'être modifiés grâce aux degrés mobiles et donc de différer d'un mode à l'autre.

Gérard Geay

BIBLIOGRAPHIE

PARTITIONS

Anonyme
- Le manuscrit H 196 de la Faculté de médecine de Montpellier, édité par Yvonne Rokseth. Éditions de l'Oiseau Lyre, Paris 1935–[1939].

Boësset, Antoine (1587–1643) ou Jean-Baptiste (1614–1685) [4]
- La Messe à quatre du 11e mode. Cahiers de musique 85, Versailles 2001.
- Les Motets à voix égales. Cahiers de musique 86, Versailles 2001.
- Les Motets à voix mixtes. Cahiers de musique 87, Versailles 2001.

Bouzignac, Guillaume (1587 ? – ?)
- La Messe à sept parties (Cette messe n'est qu'attribuée à Bouzignac). Cahiers de musique 17, Versailles 1997.
- Les volumes 1 et 2 des Motets. Cahiers de musique 61 et 62, Versailles 1998.
- Les Chansons. Cahiers de musique 63, Versailles 2001.

Boyer, Jean (? – 1648)
- Les Airs à quatre parties. Cahiers de musique 89, 99 et 100, Versailles 2003.

Du Caurroy, Eustache (1549–1609)
- les Fantaisies d'Eustache Du Caurroy. Édition de Blaise Pidoux. Institute of Mediæval Music, Brooklyn 1975.
- Preces ecclesiasticæ. Édition de Marie-Alexis Colin, en co-édition avec le Centre d'Études Supérieures de la Renaissance de Tours et les Éditions Klincksieck. Paris 2000.

Formé, Nicolas (1567–1638)
- Les œuvres complètes. Édition de Jean-Charles Léon, Versailles 2003.

Frémart, Henri (? –1651)
- Les œuvres complètes. Édition de Inge Forst, Versailles 2003.

Guédron, Pierre (1570/75 ?–1619/20 ?)
- Les airs de cour. Édition de Georgie Durosoir à paraître en 2007 aux éditions du Centre de Musique Baroque de Versailles.

Le Prince, Louis (?–?)
- La Missa Macula non est in te. Cahiers de musique 9, Versailles 2001.

---

4. Les sources ne précisant jamais le prénom, nous ne sommes pas parvenus, jusqu'à présent, à attribuer ces œuvres au père ou au fils.

Menault, Pierre (1642-1694)
- Les messes pour St Étienne de Dijon. Édition de Michel Cuvelier, Versailles 1993.
- Les vêpres à deux chœurs. Édition de Michel Cuvelier, Versailles 2004.
- La Missa Ave senior Stephane. Cahiers de musique 82, Versailles 2003.

Moulinié, Étienne (1600 ? - après 1669)
- Les Meslanges de sujets chrestiens. Édition de Jean Duron, Versailles 1996.

Nivers, Guillaume-Gabriel (1632 ? -1714)
- Livre d'orgue... Éditions J. M. Fuzeau, Courlay 1987.
- 2. Livre d'orgue... Éditions J. M. Fuzeau, Courlay 1992.
- 3. Livre d'orgue des huit tons de l'Eglise. Éditions J. M. Fuzeau, Courlay 1994.

Titelouze, Jehan (1563-1603)
- la deuxième édition des Hymnes de l'Eglise. Éditions J. M. Fuzeau, Courlay 1992.
- le Magnificat de Jehan Titelouze. Éditions J. M. Fuzeau, Courlay 1992.

TRAITÉS

Blockland de Montfort
- Instruction méthodique et fort facile pour apprendre la musique practique. Lyon 1587, Genève 1972.

Campion, François
- Traité d'accompagnement et de composition selon la règle des octaves de musique. Paris, 1716. Addition au traité d'accompagnement par la règle d'octave. Paris 1730, Genève 1976.

Caus, Salomon de
- Institution Harmonique. Francfort 1615, Genève 1980.

Glarean, Heinrich
- Dodecachordon. Bâle 1547, New York, 1969.

Ballard, Pierre
- Traicté de Musique... Paris 1617 (Nouvelle édition du traité de 1583).

La Voye Mignot, Sieur de
- Traité de musique... Paris 1656. Seconde édition. Paris 1666. Genève 1972.

Le Roy, Adrian et Ballard, Robert
- Traicté de Musique... Paris 1583.

Maillart, Pierre

- Les Tons ou Discours sur les modes de musique et les tons de l'église et la distinction entre iceux. Tournai 1610, Genève 1972.

Mersenne, Marin
- Correspondance. Paris 1932–1957.
- Harmonie Universelle, Paris 1636, Paris 1975. Volume 2. Livre qvatriesme. De la composition de mvsique. p. 197 ff.

Nivers, Guillaume-Gabriel
- Traité de la composition de mvs[i]que. Paris 1667.

Parran, Antoine
- Traité de la mvsique… Paris 1639, Genève 1972.

Yssandon, Jean
- Traité de musique pratique… Paris 1582, Genève 1972.

Zarlino, Gioseffo
- Istitutioni Harmoniche. Venetia 1558, New York 1965.
- Dimostrationi harmoniche, Venetia 1571, New York 1965.
- Istitutioni Harmoniche. Venetia 1573, New York 1966.

LITTÉRATURE

Duron, Jean (textes réunis par)
- Plain-chant et liturgie en France au XVIIe siècle. Versailles et Paris 1997.

Durosoir, Georgie
- "Au temps de Marie de Médicis", in: Le concert des muses, textes réunis par Jean Lionnet. Versailles 1997.

Gallat-Morin, Élisabeth et Pinson, Jean-Pierre
- La vie musicale en Nouvelle-France. Sillery (Québec) 2003.

Geay, Gérard
- "Contrepoint et modalité dans les airs en mineur de Guédron", in: Poésie, musique et société. L'air de cour en France au XVIIe siècle. Textes réunis par Georgie Durosoir. Versailles et Sprimont 2006, pp. 207–225.
- "Éditer Frémart et la polyphonie française du XVIIe siècle" / "Editing Frémart and French 17th-century polyphony". Translated by Mary Criswick, in: Henri Frémart, Œuvres complètes. Edition de Inge Forst. Versailles 2003, pp. XVIII-XXXIV et pp. LII-LVII
- "Modalité et plan tonal: un exemple de Henry Desmarest", in: Bulletin de l'Atelier d'Études sur la musique française des XVIIe & XVIIIe siècles. Versailles 2003.

– "Polyphonie im Frankreich des 17. Jahrhunderts. Theoretische und praktische Perspektiven", in: Ludwig Holtmeier (Editeur scientifique), Musiktheorie zwischen Historie und Systematik. 1. Kongress der Deutschen Gesellschaft für Musiktheorie in Dresden 2001. Augsburg 2004.

Guillo, Laurent
– Pierre I Ballard et Robert III Ballard, imprimeurs du roy pour la musique (1599–1673). Liège 2003.

Pinson, Jean-Pierre: voir sous Gallat-Morin, Élisabeth.

Schneider, Herbert
– Die französische Kompositionslehre in der ersten Hälfte des 17. Jahrhunderts. Tutzing 1972.

Wolf, Johannes
– Ein Beitrag zur Diskantlehre des 14. Jahrhunderts. Sammelbände der Internationalen Musikgesellschaft. Leipzig 1913–1914.

TOWARDS A HISTORY OF HARMONIC TONALITY

Susan McClary

The theories of harmonic tonality that flourished in the eighteenth century ground themselves in purely musical premises: in mathematical relationships, in the overtone series derived from physical acoustics, in systematic demonstrations such as the Rule of the Octave. Within the intellectual framework thus established, music seems to make itself up out of rational principles that exist independent of human invention. It is as though the musicians of the eighteenth century—much like contemporaneous scientists—had discerned structures of order waiting there to be discovered, once they swept the mystifications of former epistemologies aside. Not only the theories but also the music of the period appear to operate on the basis of self-contained logic, no longer subject to historical contingencies or arbitrary, expressive impulses.

Most of the essays in this volume focus on eighteenth-century theories of tonality after it has emerged as the predominant musical procedure. And rightly so, for the 1700s saw an explosion of documents celebrating this moment of European ingenuity in all areas of endeavor. Moreover, the self-consistent dimension of these constructions invites even further theorizing. It is no accident that eighteenth-century tonal theory still underlies our music pedagogy and analytical methods. As with so many Enlightenment institutions, such as scientific methods or representative democracy, harmonic tonality appears to us as a transcultural ideal that should require no external explanation or justification.

I am as much a creature of harmonic tonality as anyone else, and I scarcely need to be persuaded of its aesthetic and intellectual contributions. Yet I have spent much of my career examining the repertories of the seventeenth century. For reasons I continue to try to articulate even to myself, I have always found this earlier music extraordinarily compelling, despite (or perhaps, in part, *because* of) the fact that it resists the analytical tools with which my tonal training equipped me.

Needless to say, music theorists also flourished in the 1600s, and their work tells us a great deal about how they thought about music; they left invaluable traces of their preoccupations, their ways of grappling with the musics of both their predecessors and their contemporaries. Some of them sought to catalogue the new musical genres and instruments that began to proliferate around this time, to keep track of the technological transformations that made the profession nearly as difficult to keep up with as the computer technologies of our own day.[1] Others analyze the affective codes that allowed music to move auditors to tears, to piety, or to erotic arousal.[2] Such enterprises counted in their own time as music theories, and they often appear in the same volumes as discussions of proper part writing. They also persist in explaining mode—in large part (as we shall see) because mode itself persisted.[3]

Occasionally a theorist engages with questions and techniques that appear more congruent with our conception of music theory. For instance, Christoph Bernhard, in his treatise justifying the illicit dissonances favored by composers of the *seconda prattica*, demonstrates how to reduce complex passages to their underlying structural frameworks.[4] For the most part, however, the theoretical formulations of the seventeenth century do not address the radical changes in musical syntax, some of which would (as we know only from hindsight) eventually lead to the triumph of harmonic tonality. And where little or no verbal documentation exists I propose that we treat the music itself as a repository of historical information.

---

1. See, for instance, Michael Praetorius, whose *Syntagma Musicum* (1619) attempts to make sense of the rapidly changing musical world that surrounded him. See also Ercole Bottrigari, *Il Desiderio, overo De' concerto di varii strumenti musicali, dialogo* (1594).
2. For instance, see Thomas Morley, *A Plaine and Easie Introduction to Practicall Musicke* (1597). Monteverdi himself wrote about some of his own experiments; see his preface to his Eighth Book of Madrigals (*Madrigali Guerrieri et Amorosi*, 1638).
3. *Musurgia universalis, sive Ars magna consoni et dissoni* (1650), by the Jesuit polymath Athanasius Kircher, served as the model for modal theory in Eric Chafe, *Monteverdi's Tonal Language*, New York 1992.
4. Christoph Bernhard, "Tractatus compositionis augmentatus (n.d.)"; in: Walter Hilse (ed. and trans.), *The Treatises of Christoph Bernhard*, in: *Music Forum* III, New York 1973.

I confess that the procedures that got cast aside by the end of the seventeenth century attract me more than do those that developed into what we call tonality. For purposes of this essay, however, I will concentrate on the latter and attempt to shed light on how and why their various components came together as they did. But I also hope to show that this particular amalgamation was by no means the inevitable survivor of what had been a richly eclectic range of compositional options. I suspect that most musicians from the first three-quarters of the seventeenth century would have been astonished and even somewhat saddened to learn that their choices would have become so restricted by 1700.

Before I begin my demonstration, I want to set out my assumptions—some of which fly in the face of more standard explanations for this moment of style change. First, although we now take tonality for granted, there was no *prima facie* reason why it needed to come into being. The sixteenth and seventeenth centuries yielded musics that later repertories perhaps equal in sophistication but never surpass.[5] No one was sitting around longing for the day when their music would begin to make sense; they were not trying to become "tonal". To assume tonality's inevitability in advance and to limit our sights to those pieces that seem to qualify not only makes gibberish of earlier music but it even blocks our ability to understand why tonality emerged when and as it did. Thus instead of asking of a piece of early Baroque music "is it tonal yet?", I will seek to explain how it makes use of available materials for its particular purposes.

Second, the resources deployed in sixteenth-century modality and those characteristic of tonality are not mutually exclusive. Present-day discussions of earlier music often bracket off as "tonal" those elements that seem familiar (e.g. perfect authentic cadences), leaving as "modal" only passages that do not work according to later premises. As a consequence, these compositions appear incoherent

---

5. See my *Modal Subjectivities: Self-Fashioning in the Italian Madrigal*, Berkeley and Los Angeles 2004, for an extended treatment of sixteenth-century practice.

—as odd jumbles of progressive and reactionary features. Recall, however, that perfect authentic cadences had started to become commonplace in the fifteenth century. If they count among those elements retained in the eighteenth century, they surely had shifted their meanings and functions in their later manifestations.

Finally, I will proceed with the assumption that changes in style are driven by expressive demands. If there exists no abstract reason why tonality should have developed, plenty of historical ones do present themselves, which is why cultural contexts matter even to questions of musical process. Over the course of the seventeenth century, composers assembled the devices at hand in many different ways, only some of which resulted in music that sounds familiar to us. I propose developing models that allow for cogent, internally consistent accounts of the music as it occurs, paying attention to the aesthetic reasons why the pieces that move in the direction of tonality do so within the framework of their own range of choices.

One of the highest priorities for seventeenth-century musicians was the shaping of time. Of course, temporality always stands as a dimension of music-making. But in the 1600s, composers sought to produce radical experiences of time, alternately expanding and contracting, rushing impetuously forward only to hover in a state of apparent motionlessness. The arrangement of elements we recognize as tonality figured among these, but it operated always within contexts that also encouraged wild fluctuations or nearly flat, virtually minimalist options. I wish to ask *not* why musicians persisted in using perverse procedures but rather why they occasionally found that tonal arrangement advantageous—and also why they continued to make use of other options so long after they had "discovered" it.

To put it quite simply, composers in the seventeenth century harnessed the leading tone in order to create extended trajectories of desire. If the leading tone heralds expected closure (as it had since the *trecento* at the latest), then damming up that expectation can prolong a long-term cadence-effect. As soon as ,the leading tone appears, the acculturated ear will anticipate the implied arrival; a single pitch—the designated tonic toward which the leading tone points—becomes an object of desire, the demand for which can be sustained and intensified for as long as the leading tone pushes and the arrival delays. The myriad styles of the 1600s count as diverse implementations of this technology, which rapidly transformed virtually all existing procedures into new shapes and forms (not all them—mind you—"tonal").

Certainty and delayed gratification have become such cardinal principles in tonal music that we now define musical competence principally in those terms. Earlier periods, however, actually prized ambiguity, and leading tones tended to occur only at the last moment before cadence so as to prolong a quality of (to them, in any case) delicious undecidability. In tracing the gradual emergence of tonal procedures, we thus need to examine carefully how and why the leading tone is deployed in seventeenth-century repertories, which entails analyzing not only the formal dimensions of pieces but also their expressive and rhetorical strategies.

* * *

I will begin with a composition that still works according to sixteenth-century modal premises. Although it makes use of the leading tone, it does so intermittently and always for local purposes rather than as a given of harmonic syntax. By means of this very small sample of modal compositional strategies, I hope to throw into relief the changes that occur within the first decades of the seventeenth century.[6]

Giulio Caccini's "Amarilli, mia bella" scarcely needs an introduction. Initially published in Caccini's celebrated *Le Nuove Musiche* of 1601, it quickly became an international hit; a keyboard arrangement by Peter Philips appears, for instance, in the *Fitzwilliam Virginal Book*. Moreover, it still occupies a place of honor within vocal pedagogy. We are so accustomed to seeing it in anthologies for beginners—and to hearing their still-wobbly voices negotiat-

---

6. This single example cannot stand for the entire body of work that precedes it. See again my *Modal Subjectivities*.

ing its melody—that we may think of it as a baby piece. Few other pieces designed for babies include a graphic image of sexual penetration, however.

"Amarilli, mia bella" operates within the Hypodorian mode, transposed—as it usually is—to G, with B♭ in the key signature. In a plagal mode such as Hypodorian, the octave stretches from the fifth degree of the mode down to the octave below, with the final (marked here as a double whole note) located in the middle of the terrain.

Example 1. Hypodorian Species

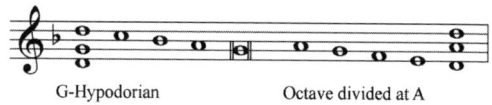

G-Hypodorian   Octave divided at A

More even than is typical of pieces in this mode, the melody of "Amarilli" stays almost exclusively within the diapente between D and G; only once does it dip down into its diatessaron (the fourth reaching from the lower D up to the final, G), but it does so in a most dramatic way. Not only does this move produce a temporary modulation suggesting D as a rival final and A rather than G as the proper divisor of the D octave, but it also produces the effect of penetration mentioned above and discussed in greater detail below.

Amarilli, mia bella,	Amarillis, my fair one,
Non credi, o del mio cor dolce desio,	Do you not believe, o sweet desire of my heart,
D'esser tu l'amor mio.	That you are my love?
Credilo pur, e se timor t'assale,	Believe it, though, and if doubt assails you
Prendi questo mio strale,	Take this, my arrow,
Aprim'il petto, e vedrai scritto in core:	Open my breast and see written on my heart:
Amarilli è'l mio amore.	Amarillis is my love.

I will concentrate on the unfolding of Caccini's melody in "Amarilli", for that is where his grammar resides. The opening section (the first ten bars) presents a series of interrupted descents from D toward G: some of the gestures halt at scale-degree 3, others at 2, but within a framework that makes its orientation toward G abundantly clear from the outset. The withheld final, G, appears finally only on "mio", thus matching the rhetorical conclusion of the lyric statement.

Example 2. Caccini, "Amarilli, mia bella", mm. 1–10

We are accustomed to tracking melodic trajectories in tonal compositions: think, for instance, of the final-movement chorale in Beethoven's Ninth Symphony or nearly any hymn or folk tune. But Caccini's *modus operandi* differs from these in the relationship between its melody and harmony. From the point of view of functional tonality, "Amarilli" plops into a modal pothole on the word "credi", and it also vacillates indecisively between G and B♭ as potential key centers.

Caccini's contemporaries, however, would have heard his harmonies as immediately comprehensible, even transparent in their implications, especially in the context of the diapente-oriented melody to which they lend their inflections. For nearly every pitch in Caccini's tune qualifies as a node of crucial modal information, each one confirmed on a one-to-one basis by harmonic support. Thus the move to F-natural in the bass on "credi" (m. 4) serves within the conventions of the day to put special stress on the melodic descent to scale-degree 4 (melodic C), which might otherwise escape notice as a mere passing tone. Moreover, the swerve to B♭ in m. 5 counts among the most powerful means of articulating the top of the G-diapente—so common as to sustain a huge body of improvisations (see below).

Because of this one-to-one relationship between fundamental pitches and harmonic changes, the music remains tethered temporally to the exigencies of the poetic phrases, allowing for an aesthetic effect Caccini (following Castiglione) labeled *sprezzatura*, similar to what we more usually call today *nonchalance*. Each lyrical phrase points in the same direction as the others, but the harmonic choices offer various shades of coloring, a spectrum of accents, before the inevitable final appears. A singer who focuses on that very low level of activity and nuance may hope to pull off the quality of aristocratic ease so valued in the Renaissance courts.

To be sure, Caccini makes use of leading tones. For instance, the harmonic F# marking the very first move ensures that we hear everything from the outset within the context of G, as does the melodic F# that follows. Indeed, this first three-bar phrase, with its consistent leading tones, could be considered tonal, though if we were to do so, we would fail to grasp Caccini's choices as significant — and we would find ourselves at sea in m. 4, when the F-natural appears in the bass. From Caccini's vantage point, those F#s freeze us into a holding position, as does his choice of weakly voiced chords on F# and E♭, for both of which he requests a sixth (not a solid fifth) above the bass. The opening phrase consequently serves to outline the terrain of the diapente, always pointing through F# to G as the final but also delaying any "real" move from the initial modal function, D, the fifth degree. Within the context of "Amarilli", this strategy counts merely as a short-term special effect, though it is precisely this ability of leading tones to prolong that will open up the new world.

Example 3. "Amarilli", mm. 1–10

Consequently, the significance of that modal pothole — the move to F-natural on "credi". If the first phrase sustains D (despite the apparent mobility of the melodic voice), the appearance of F in the bass forcibly pulls the controlling modal line down from D to C, thence to B♭ and the still-unresolved A, all articulated as genuine syntactical moments. Stopping short of the G, the melody returns to its opening position in m. 5, now harmonized with a powerful B♭ in the bass. But this time, the melodic line halts lovingly ("dolce desio") on B♭. At last, with the poetic punch line, Caccini allows for an unimpeded descent all the way from D to G. Note, however, that the quick reference to F♯ in the bass holds us up on D, while weak harmonies permit the melody to slide unimpeded down to A, which accumulates considerable gravity before it finally resolves to G in m. 10.

I have trudged laboriously through these few bars in order to tease out how Caccini wields the leading tone—as well as his other harmonic options—for purposes of inflecting his melody, which mostly remains identical with the generating modal line. He does not write "Amarilli, mia bella" as a theory exercise, however. His melody line flirts and teases, always stopping short just before divulging its secret, each time starting all over again at D but shading its approach differently. If the tortured melodic and harmonic contour of the first phrase underscores the singer's pathos, the move to C on "credi" insists on its sincerity, and the B♭ section pauses to savor Amarilli's beauty. Only the last phrase completes the message delivered so haltingly with all those fits and starts. Understanding how all those minute details signify can help the performer make this song something other than just a repetitive melody. Imagine the late Marlon Brando reciting the opening terzet with his usual self-indulgence, inserting pregnant pauses between each phrase, putting mannered emphasis on the odd word. Caccini's heavily weighted modal line choreographs just that kind of rendition.

Now for the middle section. Our speaker becomes more ardent here, pleading his case to the point where he offers an image of submission. For purposes of this argument, Caccini alternates between melodic 3 and 2, with leading tones always under the second scale degree, heating up the need for some kind of resolution. Yet regardless of the pressure, 2 remains in place, creating a kind of membrane that resists further motion. At last, recalling the success in the first section of descents from the top of the octave, the melody attempts an approach from D on "Aprim'il petto" in m. 17. But as it comes into the vicinity of the barrier pitch A, the harmonic F♯ (thus far so reliable at moments of would-be cadence) falls away in m. 19, thereby reinterpreting A as fifth degree of the lower D (confirmed by a C♯ in the accompaniment).

All the urgency aimed at transcending A suddenly breaks through into a terrain of interiority not yet even hinted at. That A becomes the surface of the body opened up for a moment of profound erotic surrender.

Example 4. "Amarilli", mm. 11–27

It lasts only for three melodic pitches: F-natural, E, D. Almost immediately, the speaker seizes onto his beloved's name and hauls himself hand over fist back to the outside world of the diapente. The ascent requires the assistance of several of what we would call secondary or applied dominants (B-natural, C#), all perfectly available and comprehensible within sixteenth-century modal practice; within this context, they contribute to the effect of intense physical effort. And in case you thought you had imagined that moment of penetration, Caccini lets us hear the entire sequence again, note for note. A brief coda elaborates a major-key plagal ("Amen") effect with E-natural blossoming out on top, before the voice concludes with a chain of ornaments to be executed deep in the back of the throat — a wordless orgasm of sorts.

Caccini's composed his songs in *Le Nuove Musiche* within a court context. He had first attracted the attention of patrons as a solo singer in Rome; when he put this collection together, he was affiliated with the Medici cultural establishment in Florence. Just the previous year, he had engaged in a sordid squabble over the invention of opera, and he had rushed his own setting of Ottavio Rinuccini's *Euridice* into print after he had recognized Jacopo Peri's original as the wave of the future. In his preface to that publication, Caccini set forth the now-familiar story of the Florentine

Camerata as a way of backing up his own claim. *Le Nuove Musiche*, with its detailed account of Caccini's celebrated performance style, meant similarly to nail down his right to having developed the new style long before Peri.[7]

But Caccini's talents lay in his ability to set lyrical verse, which (however remarkable) do not engage the innovative techniques Peri and others brought to the table. His songs served as vehicles for his own chamber performances, as well as those of his wife and daughters (including Francesca, a much-celebrated composer in her own right).[8] By publishing these songs, he also entered into the burgeoning commercial market, and his songs were evidently sung in households eager to emulate aristocratic culture. The versions of temporality and subjectivity in Caccini's songs, however, still closely resemble those of the court madrigal.

* * *

In order to track the prehistory of what gave Peri the edge in this competition, we have to turn to improvisatory practices—practices also fundamental to court culture, though different from the composed repertories to which Caccini contributed. These practices date back to periods during which no one felt the need to notate them, but they begin to appear written out in the "teach yourself to improvise" manuals that proliferated in the second half of the sixteenth century.[9] Much like the blues progression of a later time, the formulas that served as the basis for elaboration rely on the most fundamental of patterns: in this case, the diapente descent harmonized in its most powerful and straightforward ways.

---

7. See Howard Mayer Brown, "How Opera Began: An Introduction to Jacopo Peri's *Euridice*", in: Eric Cochrane (ed.), *The Late Italian Renaissance, 1525–1630*, London 1970, pp. 401–43.
8. Suzanne Cusick has explored Francesca Caccini's career and music in detail. See her "Of Women, Music, and Power: A Model from Seicento Florence", in: Ruth Solie (ed.), *Musicology and Difference*, Berkeley and Los Angeles 1993, pp. 281–304. Cusick is now completing a book on Francesca Caccini's life and works.
9. See, for instance, the *Tratado* of Diego Ortiz.

Example 5. Improvisatory patterns

Passamezzo antico

Romanesca

Note that these patterns share as their generating modal lines the same diapente descent. The *Passamezzo antico* harmonizes the fifth degree, D, with the final in the bass, making the mode fully audible right from the outset. To our ears, the second move in the progression may sound abrupt and archaic: indeed, it presents an instance of parallel fifths. Nonetheless, this progression occurs quite commonly in modal music (recall the passage discussed above in "Amarilli, mia bella"), even if composers usually work to hide the baldness of the parallels.

The *Romanesca* differs from the *Passamezzo antico* only in that it begins by harmonizing the fifth degree with a mediant in the bass. When the bass moves to F-natural this time (in support of the descent to 4), it sounds as if it is establishing B♭ as a tonic. The arrival on the third function, however, clarifies the situation by pointing to G as the final. This formula counts as the most powerful and most familiar harmonization of the G-Hypodorian diapente descent: in other words, it should not be regarded as flipping from one key (B♭) to another (G). Composers choose one or the other on the basis of strategy; with respect to modal syntax, however, they are virtually interchangeable.

We know these patterns best from a song based on them: "Greensleeves", sometimes attributed to Henry VIII. Like most other aristocratic amateurs at court, Henry at least would have known how to ring changes on these familiar formulas, whether or not he actually "composed" this particular song. The first part of "Greensleeves" unfolds over a *Passamezzo antico* harmonization, the second over the *Romanesca*. In each half, the generating

Towards a History of Harmonic Tonality

descent pauses on 2, then repeats the process for a full cadential arrival on the final.

Example 6. "Greensleeves"

What differentiates "Greensleeves" from "Amarilli, mia bella" theoretically, however, is a new level of melodic activity. Whereas nearly every pitch of Caccini's tune operates as a full-fledged function in the generating modal line, each move articulated by a new harmony, Romanesca formulas present the corresponding functions in the background; over that background, the tune we sing as "Greensleeves" flows with rhythmic and melodic freedom: it does not, in other words, just hammer four times down through the diapente (as in my reduction above), but rather spins a graceful, imaginative web. Yet we do not get lost syntactically; if we do not hear the generating modal pitches directly, we can rely on the standardized harmonic pattern to keep us oriented. Note that the harmonies in "Greensleeves" are not, except at the standard cadence, "tonal". What I referred to in the Caccini example as a modal pothole occurs right on schedule here and for exactly the same purpose: to project strongly the descent to scale-degree 4 in the generating line. The harmonies still qualify, in other words, as a secondary parameter, as elements that inflect the steps along the modal line.

The guidance of the harmonic formula absolves the singer from having to stick doggedly (as in the Caccini) to the literal presentation of the modal line. With the more widely spaced harmonic moves, this new melodic line moves around in a relatively relaxed manner. The down side (for we always lose something for every advantage in a style change) is that this kind of music-making relies heavily on formulas to make sense. Moreover, it depends — like the 12-bar blues — on a pre-set rate of harmonic rhythm: in this case, one change per measure except in the approach to the cadence. But by means of those formulas, the melody of "Greensleeves" can range from its lower D in the first strain to the F a tenth above in the second. We are no longer grammatically required to specify a plagal or authentic arrangement of species, for this mechanism operates solely on the basis of a generating diapente. The melodic pitches that emerge to configure the sung tune qualify as ornamental with respect to syntax.

* * *

Jacopo Peri excelled as an improviser within such formulas. Even his contribution to the 1589 Medici wedding festivities — the lavishly decorated "Dunque fra torbide onde" — operates according to this model, as does the celebrated "Possente spirto" from Monteverdi's *Orfeo* (1607). When Peri turned his hand to writing the speech-like recitations for *Euridice*, he brought with him, as though by second nature, this double-level sense of melodic activity, and he used it to produce the highly directed yet easy-going style of recitation that made *Euridice* a historically significant event. As Howard Mayer Brown has demonstrated, Caccini failed to grasp the foundation of Peri's technique, and his re-settings of Rinuccini's speeches stagnate in rudderless monotony.[10]

But Claudio Monteverdi, an artist then famed for his polyphonic madrigals, more than met Peri's challenge in *Orfeo*. A veritable compendium of compositional possibilities available at the moment, this *favola per musica* boasts every device Monteverdi had ever employed, plus those Peri had thrown onto the stage. In contrast to Caccini, Monteverdi figured out how Peri accomplished his trick. After a prologue, in which he displays his ability

---

10. Brown, "How Opera Began", cf. n. 7.

to turn out variations over a set formula, he opens his first act with a dazzling instance of the new *stile recitativo* as a shepherd exhorts his companions to join in celebrating Orfeo's marriage.

In questo lieto e fortunato giorno	On this happy, fortunate day
ch'ha posto fine a gl'amorosi affanni	that puts an end to the amorous longings
del nostro semideo,	of our demigod,
cantiam, pastori, in sì soavi accenti	let's sing, shepherds, in such sweet accents
che sian degni d'Orfeo nostri concenti.	as will make our strains worthy of Orfeo.

Our shepherd's speech derives its directionality from Monteverdi's use of a single diapente descent in the background: the entire statement occurs under the umbrella of that powerful trajectory.[11] In that sense, it merely harnesses the energies available within the familiar *Romanesca*-type formulas to perform its rhetorical task. In contrast to a standard, evenly paced *Romanesca*, however, Monteverdi dictates the rate of change in the background. The kind of melodic flexibility already noted in "Greensleeves" here becomes even more elastic, as the composer determines how quickly to proceed through the standard progression, and the degree of expansion increases enormously.

Example 7. Monteverdi, Orfeo: *"In questo lieto e fortunato giorno"*

---

11. This is only the opening section, which repeats again after a more discursive middle section. The middle part proceeds through a number of very interesting maneuvers of the sort I will deal with elsewhere. For now, I want to concentrate on the expansion of the diapente formula alone.

For instance, Monteverdi prolongs the initial fifth degree, A, for over half the length of the entire speech. He begins by harmonizing it through alternations between D and A in the bass, thus producing a holding position. No leading tones occur here, for this is not a cadential situation. But that very indeterminacy allows the melodic line to move sometimes through B♭ to circumscribe A as the upper boundary of D (m. 2), at other times through B-natural to imply A as a potential final (m. 3). Monteverdi's holding position matches, of course, Alessandro Striggio's rhetorical ploy, which gets our attention but then defers delivering its message until the arrival of the words "cantiam, Pastori".[12] At this point, Monteverdi reharmonizes his still-reigning A with the mediant in the bass, and with this *Romanesca* rendering of the fifth degree he commences his more or less straightforward diapente descent.

But, of course, we do not hear this display as compositional experimentation but rather as the speech delivered by a character in an opera. By means of this quite audacious expansion effect, the shepherd reveals himself as an orator worthy of belonging to Orfeo's entourage. He has not been hanging around with this rhetorical demigod, son of Apollo, for nothing; he has picked up some of the boss's techniques along the way.

Orfeo's wedding song, "Rosa del ciel", begins with an even riskier strategy in which he hurls an extended apostrophe to the sun over a single sustained pitch in the bass. As I have argued elsewhere, Orfeo thereby commands the very sun (that is, Apollo) to stand still until he releases it with the verb of his main clause.[13] The rhetorical control required for meeting this challenge translated into personal power in the Renaissance courts that so treasured oratorical skill. We do not have to be told explicitly why Orfeo has acquired so much clout: we hear it with our own ears, as he sweeps us into his thrall during his wedding vows.

---

12. Compare this with the tactic opening Milton's *Paradise Lost*: "Of Man's First Disobedience, and the Fruit / Of that Forbidden Tree, whose mortal tast / Brought Death into the World, and all our woe, / With loss of *Eden*, till one greater Man / Restore us, and regain the blissful Seat, / SING, Heavenly Muse!"
13. See "Constructions of Gender in Monteverdi's Dramatic Music", in my *Feminine Endings: Music, Gender, and Sexuality*, Minneapolis ²2002, Chapter 2.

Clearly, Orfeo's deputy — our shepherd who opens Act I with "In questo lieto e fortunato giorno" — cannot rival his mentor. Still, his own exhibit of rhetorical prowess identifies him as the spokesperson of the shepherds, as a character with a degree of social prestige second only to Orfeo's. As Suzanne Cusick has demonstrated, the Medici were so jealous of the simulation of power afforded by the *stile recitativo* that they wanted to be recognized as the source of the energies generated by these devices. Consequently, much of the monodic music produced in their court remains anonymous, making it difficult to establish with certainty who actually composed it.[14] The widespread perception of these expansion devices as performances of power explain in large part why such apparently simple mechanisms suddenly took over the whole field.

Although they enable a radically new temporality, the harmonic changes in "In questo lieto e fortunato giorno" operate according to modal convention: they still serve to articulate the moves — or to delay motion — in the modal line. Those two opening harmonies that rock back and forth under the sustained A do not qualify as tonic and dominant: they are but harmonizations of 5 on the final and the fifth degree, with the one on the fifth degree refusing to tip its hand with a leading tone until the penultimate chord for a standard cadential formula.

But *Orfeo* also offers up some instances of tonal strategy. Orfeo himself opens Act II with a little song in which he celebrates his marriage. A dance-like lyrical piece, "Ecco pur" unfolds over an active, rhythmically shifting bass line rather than the sustained-note bass of the shepherd's speech-oriented "In questo". Moreover, the harmonies all work to circumscribe a succession of local key areas, each with its requisite leading tone. As it turns out, the succession itself traces the familiar *Romanesca* background. But now each node along the way becomes a tiny tonic in its own right.

---

14. Cusick, forthcoming book.

> Ecco pur ch'a voi ritorno,
> care selve e piagge amate,
> da quel sol fatte beate
> per cui sol mie notti han giorno.
>
> Behold, I return to you,
> dear woods and beloved hills,
> made blissful by that sun through which
> alone my nights have day.

If "Greensleeves" and "In questo" offered an added melodic level in its expansion, "Ecco pur" presents also another level of harmonic activity: one still marking the modal progression in the background, the other sustaining each point in the background through cadential harmonies. I will define this particular hierarchical configuration as tonal, insofar as it makes use of circumscriptive chords to sustain each moment along the way in a single, non-redundant teleological progression. In "Ecco pur", all parameters point forward to implied conclusions: the background to its arrival on the final, the surface harmonies to cadential confirmation of the immediate tonic. However brief this song may be, it operates according to fully tonal premises.

Example 8. Orfeo: *"Ecco pur"*

Because the background still lies very close to the surface, however, we ought to be able to hear the effort exerted in keeping each moment going until the eventuality of the next. For example, the harmonies strongly suggest closure at the beginning of m. 2. Only the infusion of additional energy produced in the voice's sudden leap from the final, G, up to D prevents the piece from ending almost before it has begun. Against what Monteverdi stages as great difficulty, Orfeo's melody delays the arrival until m. 4: the friction between harmony and melody in mm. 2–3 derive from Orfeo's resistance to what would otherwise be just a chain of parallel sixths (C/E♭, B♭/D, A/C) pulling forcefully down through the diapente to the cadence on G. None of these would qualify as "real" moves in modality; they participate as middle-level devices in the prolongation. Rhetorically, however, this passage offers the impression that Orfeo defies even the gravitational pull of cadential harmonies, as he puts a drag on each step, finally allowing the cadence to occur only when he deems fit.

A four-measure-long prolongation may not impress us much, given the epic expansions of, say, Bruckner. But it all starts here—with the pitting of cadential harmonies against their own fundamental tendencies. A pattern that arouses the expectation for closure produces a spark of energy that a composer can harness for extension. The desire for closure—indeed, the assumption that it always lies nearly within our grasp—cannot ever be allowed to dissipate; it has to be channeled by means of middle-level tactics such as the ones just discussed.

Note that the cadential premise announces itself with the appearance of the leading tone, signaling the arrival on melodic 2. This is why most of the activity within closed key areas concentrates on the vacillation between 3 and 2, with the tonic or final withheld until the point of closure. Accordingly, a Schenkerian analyst might well read the opening key area of "Ecco pur" as sustaining 3 rather than 5, as in my reduction. But however much my reductions may resemble Schenker graphs, they have a rather different purpose: namely, to demonstrate the gradual emergence of tonal procedures from earlier ones. In 1607, a descent from 3 would make little grammatical sense—a modal analyst would always seek the generating 5. As the expanded steps of the diapente descent become standard modulatory schemata, however, the interest for composer and analyst alike properly gets transferred to the middle ground—to strategies for simultaneously maintaining and postponing.

The question of whether "Ecco pur" qualifies as tonal really depends upon the degree of prolongation one requires. Like the other pieces just discussed, it is based syntactically on a descent through a minor-mode diapente. I use the term "minor mode" because the diapente of Dorian and Aeolian have identical interval structures; the same is true of Mixolydian and Ionian. So long as all activity occurs only within the species of fifth (as in "Ecco pur"), we have only two procedures: major and minor. Moreover, each point along the diapente descent in "Ecco pur" features nothing but cadential prolongations. None of the ambiguities or exploitations of modally sensitive pitches beloved of Monteverdi and his colleagues in other contexts (including the rest of *Orfeo*) arise here. Still, each "key" is so brief that it hardly warrants our opting for an entirely different brand of analysis, especially when "Ecco pur" can be understood more fruitfully from a vantage point that makes it consistent with the other movements in the opera.

Consequently, I prefer to hear this little aria as performing a particular rhetorical role, which returns us to the issue of power. Orfeo's fake-out at the beginning of m. 2 (where he suddenly pulls away the cadence in which he seems to have acquiesced) and his series of dragged resistances against the bass in the next two measures contribute immeasurably to his aura of personal charisma. Those cadential harmonies want to slam the door shut, but he inserts himself as a sonorous wedge, preventing — or at least postponing — the gratification of closure until he can do it his way.

* * *

I want to flash forward about forty years for my final example: the opening section of Antonio Cesti's chamber cantata "Pose in fronte". In that little aria, Cesti manages to extend his diapente descent for 44 measures, as each step of the descent balloons up to the length of a full-fledged key area by means of cadential harmonies. The dynamic tension between surface and background remains quite palpable: repeatedly the harmonies try to cadence, only to have the melody refuse immediate gratification, demanding a renewed pursuit of the goal.

Like many mid-century pieces trafficking so obviously with dammed up desire, Cesti's cantata presents an explicitly masochistic scenario. The final aria simply murmurs over and over "I love the arrows and adore the chains". This opening segment, however, has the task of whipping up the energies that will carry the entire multi-section composite to its languid, satiated conclusion. And for this purpose Cesti employs the most teleological devices he knows.

Example 9. Cesti, "Pose in fronte," movement 1

Pose in fronte al mio tiranno	Proud Love set chains and arrows
fiero Amor catene e strali;	down in front of my tyrant;
queste schiavo il cor mi fanno,	the former enslave my heart,
quei mi dan piaghe mortali.	The latter give me mortal pangs.

The cantata starts with a brief continuo introduction: a slightly elaborated tetrachord descent from B to F# in the bass. When the voice enters, the bass attempts to repeat its easy confirmation of tonic, and at m. 8 both parts appear poised to cadence; one has only to allow the voice to descend to B, and we would be off and running toward the next goal. But instead, the bass veers off to D# (leading tone to an implied E), driving the voice up to cry out "proud Love" in its high register. With the reappearance of A# in the voice and F# in the bass, we seem once again on the brink of closure on B. This time, however, the melody refuses to comply with the powerful arrival in the continuo. Marshalling all its energies, it pulls itself up—apparently dragging the bass up with it—to a definitive cadence in m. 17.

In order to mark this as an arrival, Cesti disrupts the *moto perpetuo* of his *bel canto* triple meter with a hemiola pattern. Still, the voice has virtually no time to revel in that accomplishment, for the following beat announces the move forward to the next stage in the background—D major—and the first of two settings of the second two lines of text. Like many arias of this period, "Pose in fronte" unfolds in an ABB' formal schema, whereby the initial section sets out the tonic key area and the opening lines of text while the second moves twice through the remaining text, accomplishing whatever secondary key areas the composer wishes to touch upon before returning to tonic for ultimate closure. For this particular aria, Cesti chooses to remain within a single, harmonically stable (though rhythmically turbulent) key the first time through. What might have produced an arrival in m. 20 gets finessed, as the voice pushes onward, extending this key area forcibly until m. 26.

The reiteration of these same two lines proves rather more intricate, however, even though it does work its way back to the closing tonic. For fast on the heels of the D-major cadence in m. 26 comes what first seems a return to tonic, which could materialize as soon as m. 31. But the bass delivers a deceptive sixth degree in place of the expected B. Moreover, the melody flips up to E, which maneuvers the piece into a circumscribed area on A: the typical Romanesca harmonization of scale-degree 4 with subtonic in the bass and the announcement of a genuine descent from the background fifth degree, which has been sustained by both B minor and D major. The descent continues to 3 in the modal line, harmonized first with F#, then with G, with the voice's abject C-natural seeming to concede to yet another key area before a last-ditch effort pulls us back to the safety of C# (2) and a final, hemiola-marked cadence on B. The continuo rounds out the aria by repeating its framing ritornello.[15]

Example 10. "Pose," reduction

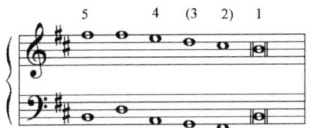

To sing this aria, one is literally forced to become breathless, panting urgently after every designated goal, only to be goaded mercilessly on to the next. Both performer and listener are hurled forward in time, the present moment never anything more than a prod toward the ever-retreating future. Only when the final itself appears as the goal does the trajectory come to some sort of halt — a halt that within this style always sounds provisional and even artificial, despite the broadening effect of the hemiola. For once the desire machine gets wound up, it proves very hard to shut it down, to make any particular prize sound commensurate with what had compelled us there. In this case, the prize sought after so fervently and with so much genuine heavy breathing is a B. No big deal — until it becomes grist for the mill of tonality.

* * *

---

15. Note that many seventeenth-century arias — even those as late as Stradella's — have different beginning and ending ritornelli, the first corresponding to the materials of the opening A section, the second to the closing materials. This structural plan yields a sense of progress in that it implies its unfolding has resulted in actual change. By contrast, the da Capo aria (among the first formal conventions based on tonal solid premises) reinforces the centrality of its tonic by reiterating the same ritornello at the beginning and close of the A section — and then again when the A section returns following the contrasting middle part. This is tonal control with a vengeance, which befits a genre overwhelmingly concerned with decorum and absolutist power.

Everything necessary for the pursuit of tonality exists at this point. In their respective pieces, Monteverdi and Cesti not only make use of functional harmony, but they also reveal that they grasp the concept of hierarchical nesting: the process that would enable the repertories of the next three hundred years. If only seventeenth-century composers had recognized the potential of "Ecco pur" or "Pose in fronte" immediately! Alas, historical events rarely unfold in such a straightforward fashion. Indeed, the middle sections of Cesti's cantata exploit the erratic moves of his still fully operative Aeolian (*not* minor) mode: they do not begin and end in the same key but simulate instead the ambivalences of a tormented, self-divided subject. Only the opening section, which sets the stage, qualifies as tonal — and even here, the Neapolitan in m. 37 undermines the strength of this temporary tonic arrival, pointing forward to subsequent sections.

In other words, Monteverdi, Cesti, and their colleagues understood perfectly well what to do with the expansion procedures just discussed. But they persisted in treating them as tools they could implement when they deemed them appropriate for their particular rhetorical purposes. As it turns out, they continued for several decades to work within the structures already familiar to them from the madrigal, expanding some moments melodically, others by means of circumscriptive harmonic devices. Sometimes even as late as Bach or Vivaldi a passage of intensive expansion will give way to part of the background line that presents itself *as the surface*, with no elaboration whatsoever.[16]

Seventeenth-century composers used expansion devices much as a photographer might a zoom lens. At any moment, the listener must be prepared for a radical change of temporal orientation. Thus in order to follow their strategies, we need to have at hand — as did they — the potential complexities of modal structures, as well as a number of special operations that allowed for various degrees of expansion.

In short, tonality does not actually supplant modality. Mode continues to provide the background of successive modulations

---

16. See my discussion of Vivaldi in "What Was Tonality?", in: *Conventional Wisdom: The Content of Musical Form*, Berkeley and Los Angeles 2000, Chapter 3.

that lends a sense of inevitable *telos* to formally closed sections and also to supply the logical connections among the series of sections, most of which cannot qualify as autonomous movements. Functional tonality then constitutes but one way of construing the available resources. Moreover, for much of the seventeenth century, it fails even to count as the most popular of the options.[17]

In closing I want to consider some of the reasons for tonality's eventual prevalence at the expense of all other contenders. First, tonality counts as one of several moves toward the formal standardization that enables greater transparency of communication in the 1700s. Ellen Rosand has shown how the pressures of quickly providing music for commercial opera in Venice in the 1640 (like the writers of film music, the composers came in at the last minute to set full-length plays) encouraged the widespread adoption of pre-set conventions such as tonality.[18] If Monteverdi had the luxury of creating complex allegories within his musical settings, the genre tended to follow the model of Francesco Cavalli, who figured out how to streamline his process by means of formulas like the ones we have just examined. Moreover, as publishers started to extend their markets to target a burgeoning merchant class, the intelligibility of sonatas such as those of Arcangelo Corelli, which likewise stick to these formulaic backgrounds, proved unexpectedly profitable. The expanded diapente thus became the procedure of choice in part owing to commercial pressures and marketability.

Second, the secularization of urban cultures that followed in the wake of religious wars had the effect of marginalizing the mysticism that had been so prominent in nearly all religions earlier in the seventeenth century. Although we may regard those mystical movements as reactionary, they inspired some of the most avant-garde music of the time, including that of Monteverdi, Alessandro

---

17. I deal with these other options in *Power and Desire in Seventeenth-Century Music* (University of California Press, in progress).
18. Ellen Rosand, *Opera in Seventeenth-Century Venice: The Creation of a Genre*, Berkeley and Los Angeles 1991.

Grandi, Heinrich Schütz, and many others. In the interest of producing experiences associated with Divine Union, composers sought to warp time and to simulate out-of-body sensations — nearly anything but the regulated temporalities of tonality.

Recall, for instance, the elevation toccatas of Girolamo Frescobaldi, in which leading tones point erratically in ever shifting directions, thereby dramatizing the moment during Communion of the Transubstantiation of wine into blood; significantly, the device usually aligned with human reason here produce vectors of disorientation in the face of the ineffability of Divine Truth. Or think of all the shocking sacred monodies that make use of sexual imagery to portray religious bliss. But with the decline of these sentiments within important cultural centers, the motivation for pursuing such musical strategies also drained away. One can find vestiges of mystical pietism and its musical analogues, however, in the music of J. S. Bach — a composer who became an ardent convert to the tonality of Vivaldi but who still reverted more often than is usually recognized to the ecstasies of his predecessors. Vestiges in particular of Frescobaldi's explorations of irrationality continue to show up throughout Bach's career.

Third, the influence of French classical aesthetics on courts throughout Europe involved, among other things, the cleaning up of wilful and irrational musical strategies. The sex farces of the Venetian stage get pushed aside by the far more dignified — and intensely codified — genre of *opera seria*. And the quirky fits and starts of mid-century violin sonatas give way to more dignified principles of organization. Does the widespread acceptance of aesthetic values such as *modération* and *raison* borrowed from the Absolutist court count entirely as progress? As a reminder of what underlay those values, see Robert Isherwood's *Music in the Service of the King* or Norbert Elias's *The Court Culture*.[19] The formal rigidity of *opera seria* and of tonal process might even qualify as a

---

19. Robert Isherwood, *Music in the Service of the King*, Ithaca 1973; Norbert Elias, *The Court Society*, trans. Edmund Jephcott, New York 198). See also Kathryn Hoffmann, *Society of Pleasures: Interdisciplinary Readings in Pleasure and Power During the Reign of Louis XIV*, New York 1997.

reaction formation, reining in the idiosyncratic extravagances of seventeenth-century musical expression.

Finally, tonality fits perfectly within the ideological framework of the Enlightenment, with its emphasis on ideals such as Reason, social regulation, the possibility of self-fashioning without reference to contingency. It is because of such features that tonal music submits so perfectly to the enterprises of music theory, which sought to celebrate and render explicit the principles that allowed for simulations of pure logic. I hasten, moreover, to stress that this repertory performed very complex cultural work: the eighteenth century did not simply sacrifice beauty and expressivity on the altar of convention.[20]

Yet the emergence of tonality cannot count as an obvious development, even if—*especially* if—theorists at the time worked to erase its historical tracks and to posit it as somehow natural. It may be easy to accept tonality as inevitable if we know of no viable alternatives for making musical sense. But there were. Knowing these alternatives can help us understand not only the music of the seventeenth-century *interregnum*, but also the reasons why the eighteenth so preferred tonal strategies that it expunged the memory of any other ways of being.

---

20. See my discussion in "What Was Tonality?", cf. n. 16.

TOWARDS A HISTORY OF THE ORIGIN AND DEVELOPMENT OF THE RULE OF THE OCTAVE

Markus Jans

The history of the Rule of the Octave is inseparably connected to the history of thoroughbass. The Rule of the Octave plays an essential role in both playing practice and composition, two clearly distinguishable aspects of thoroughbass.

In the early eighteenth century, as documented in theoretical works and written-out scores, thoroughbass is first and foremost an instruction for playing, giving the accompanist guidelines for improvising and elaborating on the basis of a code reduced to a bass line and occasional figures. In addition to this primarily technical level, there are a number of aesthetic specifications to be considered: place of origin, time, genre and affect ultimately lead to a great variety of performance styles.[1]

Beginning in the late sixteenth century, playing practice increasingly influences the ways in which composers think and conceive. Thoroughbass becomes a blueprint for composition, so to speak. Heinrich Schütz refers to this when he says: "Es ist bekand und am Tage, das nach dem der über den *Bassum Continuum* concertirende *Stylus Compositionis* aus Italia auch uns Deutschen zu Gesichte kommen und in die Hände gerathen, derselbige gar sehr von uns beliebet worden ist…"[2] Schütz continues by saying that anyone wishing to become a composer should, however, first be trained in traditional counterpoint.

---

1. These differentiations have been subject to research over the last twenty-five years. The results were made available and the performance practice of the music of the seventeenth and eighteenth centuries has been deeply influenced and changed. Pioneer work has been done by Jesper Christensen (Basle), and is carried on by numerous others, prominently among them Thérèse de Goede (Amsterdam).
2. From the *Vorrede zur geistlichen Chormusik,* 1648: "It is known that the style of composition which 'concerts' over the thoroughbass has come from Italy to us Germans and has become very popular."

In 1728, exactly sixty years after Schütz' text, Johann David Heinichen gives his great work on thoroughbass the following title: *Der General-Bass in der Composition, oder Neue und gründliche Anweisung, wie ein Music-Liebender mit besonderem Vortheil, durch die Principia der Composition, nicht allein den Generalbass im Kirchen-, Kammer und Theatralischen Stylo vollkommen und in altiori gradu erlernen; sondern auch zu gleicher Zeit in der Composition selbst wichtige Profectus machen könne.* In order to learn how to play thoroughbass, one must first understand the principles of composition. An experienced player will in turn progress to a higher level as a composer. While referring to the mutual permeation of practice and composition, Heinichen leaves no doubt that the two aspects can and must be separated, and furthermore, that thoroughbass contains the principles of composition.

These principles and their history are the center of focus in the following exposé. I intend to show elements of historical composition techniques which ultimately lead to the logic of sound progression as it is formulated and summed up in the various Rules of the Octave. I shall do this by means of historic "snapshots", characteristic moments in the development which has taken place over the course of the past centuries. I begin with the discussion of the Rules of the Octave.

Among the following examples there are four variants of octave rules. Ex. 1 contains two versions from *L'armonico prattico al cimbalo* (1708) by Francesco Gasparini.[3] Ex. 3 is taken from the abovementioned treatise by Johann David Heinichen. Ex. 4 is an extract from the *Traité d'harmonie réduite à ses principes naturels* (1722) by Jean-Philippe Rameau.[4]

---

3. English translation by Frank Stillings in *Music Theory Translations Series 1*, New Haven and London 1963.
4. English translation by Philip Gossett, New York 1971. A short version of the essentials of Rameau's theory was written by Jean le Rond d'Alembert in *Elémens de musique théorique et pratique suivant les principes de Monsieur Rameau*, Paris 1752. A German translation of d'Alemberts text was provided by Friedrich Wilhelm Marpurg in *Herrn d'Alembert.... Systematische Einleitung in die Musikalische Setzkunst, nach den Lehrsätzen des Herrn Rameau*, Leipzig 1757.

(Towards a History of) the Rule of the Octave

Ex. 6 is a composite of mine. All the different variants are historically authentic. I added the harmonic degrees in Roman numerals, and associated these with the harmonic functions according to Riemann's "Klangvertretung". This I did not because I approve of the obsessive tonic relatedness of Riemann's system, but rather in order to provide a synopsis for those readers who are not familiar with the Rule of the Octave, but educated and experienced in systematic harmony.

Example 1   *a) and b) from p. 34 :*

c) from p. 92:

d)

Gasparini makes a clear distinction between beginning, ending and in-between chords. An intermediary ending chord may be followed by another beginning chord, as in the combination of two fourths in fig. a). In fig. b) a fifth and a fourth are put together to complete the octave, the intermediary end and the new beginning coincide.

Fig. c) presents Gasparini's practice formula. After a brief overview of these examples we can establish a first rule: beginning notes as well as (intermediary and final) goal notes are to be played with

3-5 chords; all the ones in between, however, with 3-6 chords, regardless of how far apart the beginning and the end are. One could, in fact, imagine a case in which the extremes lay exactly an octave apart as shown in fig. d).

Instead of simple 3-6 chords, Gasparini's practice formula also features an occasional 3-5-6 or a 2-4-6 chord. The dissonances are additional ingredients. These are spiced-up sixth chords, so to speak, the inbuilt dissonance enhancing the "moving tendency" or *tendere*[5] and making the "hearing expectation" more precise: while the simple 3-6 chord leaves us with a multiple choice of possible continuations, a 5-6 chord ordinarily calling for a step up, and a 2-4-6 chord for a step down in the bass. It may be no coincidence that Gasparini uses the 5-6 chord on the fourth degree of the ascending scale, thus enforcing the *tendere* right before reaching the first goal, thus defining the "hearing expectation" and therefore giving the next chord more weight and importance. The use of the 2-4-6 chord on the fourth degree of the descending scale accelerates the motion and clarifies the direction of movement.

These dissonances in the sixth chords can be traced back to various different contrapuntal situations. I assembled a few in Ex. 2, including both passing notes and suspensions in the two-voice skeleton. Fig. a) shows situations for the 3-5-6, fig. b) for the 3-4-6 and fig. c) for the 2-4-6 chord.

Example 2   a)   b)

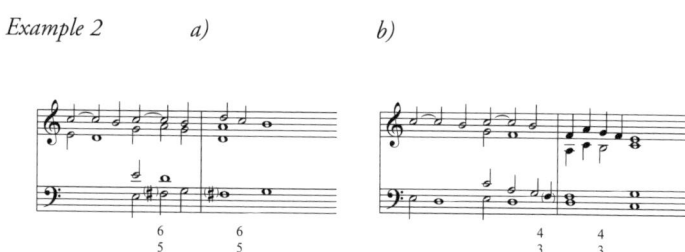

---

5. *Tendere* is a term from the fourteenth century, used to describe the "moving tendency" of an imperfect consonance toward a perfect one, often enhanced by Musica Ficta in order to let one of the two voices move a minor second, thus creating a leading tone. I will from here on use the term in a broader sense, including all the various means to create and enhance the "moving tendency" of chords.

c)

Gasparini's major scale formula shows another important feature: high-altered sixths above the sixth degree descending to the fifth, marked with asterisks as optional. This, too, is an element which enhances the *tendere*, here in the very original sense of Musica Ficta. Needless to say, these alterations also clarify the "hearing expectation".

Example 3   a) and b) from pp.747 and 748:

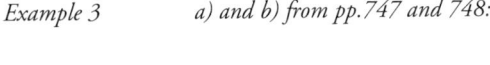

c)

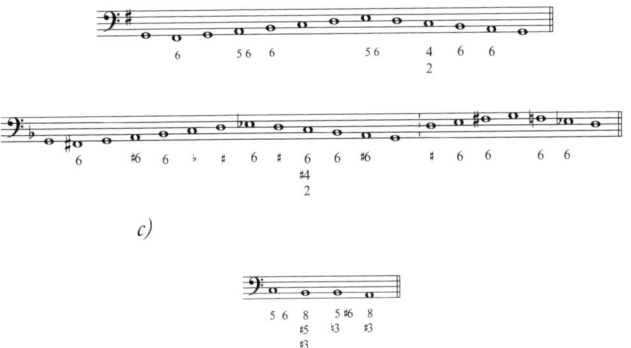

Heinichen divides the scale of the octave into two fourths. The fourth and fifth degrees are considered "goal", respectively "new start", in the ascending scale, and are therefore to be played with a 3-5 chord. Like Gasparini, Heinichen uses the 2-4-6 chord on the fourth degree in the descending scale. Of special interest are the 5-6 passages on the second and sixth degree in the major scale. This "double use"[6] is better known in connection with stepwise ascending or descending start-goal progressions, as shown in fig. c). Heinichen's suggestion may surprise us, because in the given context such progressions occur less often than the simple 3-6 chord.

---

6. I believe this constellation to be the origin and reason for Rameau's *double emploi*.

Looking at Gasparini and Heinichen together, one can state that the degrees two, three, six and seven are to be played with a 3-6 chord in both the ascending and descending scale. The fourth degree usually carries a 3-6 chord as well; in the ascending scale it may, however, also be played with a 3-5 chord and thus be made an intermediary goal. The same can be said of the sixth degree, if used in a deceptive cadence. In some cases the simple 3-6 chords may be "sharpened" by a dissonance and, according to the desired direction, be made a 2-5-6, a 3-4-6 or a 2-4-6 chord. Ficta may be used to enhance the moving tendency to an (intermediary or final) goal.

Example 4 from p. 384   a)

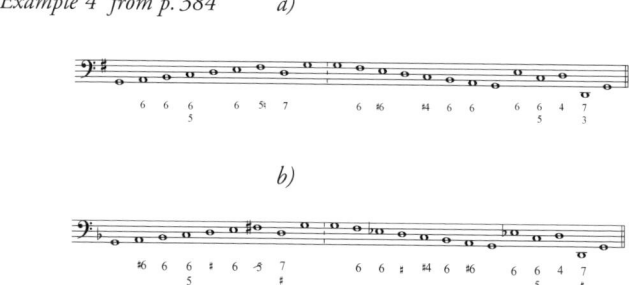

b)

The above-mentioned principles can easily be recognized in Rameau's exercise formulas as well. A new device is the leap from the seventh to the fifth and from there to the first degree. The fifth degree is to be played with a 3-5-7 chord, the seventh being prepared by the *fausse quinte* in the previous chord. The descending scale is complemented by a cadence formula.

The seventh chord resolving by a leap in the bass deserves an explanation. There are, as far as I can see, two different historic *raisons d'être* to be mentioned:

Example 5   a)

b)

(Towards a History of) the Rule of the Octave

1. The first and most important evidence is found in the two-voice intervallic progression from a suspended seventh to a sixth as shown in Ex. 5, fig. a). Sixteenth-century rules allow a variant of this progression. The "innocent" voice may, instead of waiting patiently for the dissonant one to resolve, move on. It should, however, make sure that the resolving consonance is still an imperfect one. As a result, the seventh is resolved to the third (fig. b). The multiple use of this progression leads to the *Quintfallsequenz*, and may be seen as its origin (fig. b). In some cases, the "innocent" voice may also ascend stepwise, thus resolving to a fifth (fig. c). Although the juxtaposition of a dissonance and a perfect consonance is against the hierarchic order of the intervals and therefore unwanted in the sixteenth century, there are a good number of examples to be found for this progression, too. The three possibilities of resolving the suspended seventh certainly form the basis for Rameau's *cadence parfaite (b), cadence rompue (c)* and *cadence interrompue (a)*, as shown in fig. d.).

2. In fig.e) the seventh chord occurs at the moment of resolution of a previous suspension. It is a well-known example by

Monteverdi.[7] Fig. f) shows probable steps leading to Monteverdi's formulation.

Example 6

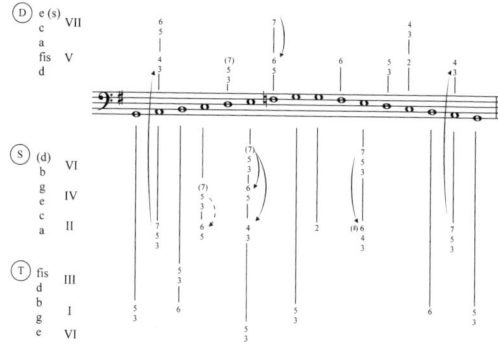

Ex. 6 contains a multitude of information. On the far left-hand side I put letters standing for the harmonic functions, with the dominant in the topmost position, the subdominant in the middle and the tonic at the bottom. Right next to these there are letters referring to pitches, written above one another. Each of the functions is accompanied by its own "tower of thirds", containing the main and the substituting chords, according to Riemann's *Klangvertretung*. The Roman numerals on the right codify the very same information in the sense of *Stufentheorie*. For the G-major ascending and descending scale I give several variants of figuring, which I graphically attribute to the functions. Some of the variants can be used only in specific sequences. Wherever this is the case, I indicate the continuation with a arrow. This concerns especially the 7-6 progressions or seventh chords which need to resolve to a sixth chord. (Or, as shown above, could be used as platforms for the bass from which to continue with a leap.) The example shows the major scale only. The minor scale variant can be obtained by simple analogy (using the high altered sixth and seventh degree for the ascending scale).

---

7. From the Madrigal Cruda Amarilli, No.1 in the Fifth Madrigal Book from 1605, m.13, "ahi lasso". The passage is quoted and heavily criticised by Artusi in his treatise on the Imperfettioni della moderna musica, Venice 1600.

(Towards a History of) the Rule of the Octave

The choice of different chords given here is, as mentioned above, historically authentic,[8] and represents the highest statistical frequency. It does, however, by no means cover all possible cases. Generally speaking, any ascending 3-6 chord may be made a 3-5-6 or a 3-4-6 chord, and any descending sixth chord may be made a 3-4-6 or a 2-4-6 chord, also depending on whether the following chord is supposed to be a 3-6 chord or a 3-5 chord. Two dissonant chords of the same kind may be used in a row. Ex. 7 shows some of the most frequently-occurring cases.

Example 7

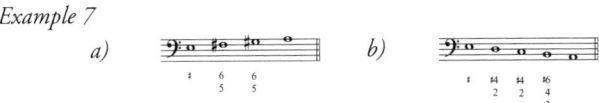

It is difficult to make a functional analysis of these progressions. Intermediary functions without their correlates would be needed, and still not explain the actual musical circumstance, being far remote from the logic which the ear and the mind perceive. A comparison of systematic harmony with the mechanics of sound progression, as exemplified in the various Rules of the Octave, is most likely to make the limitations of the first evident, a very worthwhile subject matter of its own, but not to be dealt with here.

The option to use Musica Ficta to enhance the *tendere* is open as a matter of principle in all cases in which an unstable chord is moved to a stable or, at least, a less unstable one. Any minor sixth moving to an octave can be made a major sixth, any major third led to a unison can be made a minor third, any fifth which is moved to a third can me made a diminished fifth, any fifth going to a sixth can be made an augmented fourth. The following examples are quoted from Francesco Geminiani's treatise.[9]

---

8. Documented in both compositions and theoretical works.
9. The richest in variants of this sort is certainly Geminiani's collection of Rules of the Octave, in *The Art of Accompaniment or a new and well digested method to learn to perform the THOROUGH BASS on the harpsichord, with Propriety and Elegance*, 1754, edited by Laura Alvini in *Monumenta Musica Revocata*, Firenze 1990, Vol. 1, pp. 18–24.

Example 8   *a)*

         b)

Norm or normalcy is a concept of our mind, made mainly on the basis of recurring patterns. We perceive the statistically most frequent as a point of reference, against which anything else is measured. Anything which does not conform is identified either as an error, or as an exception with a rhetorical purpose, or — if itself recurring — as a stylistic idiosyncrasy which may eventually become the norm for a new way of expression. The broader our knowledge of a specific style, the more precise our understanding of its intrinsic order, its grammar, its syntax and its rhetorics, in a word: its idiom. The theoretical description of that which we perceive as idiomatic should be as open and flexible as possible.

The simple as well as the extended Rules of the Octave provide descriptions of a basic order which are indeed open and flexible. Even though the practice formulas of the different schools give the impression of a system rather than a flexible order, considering the sum of all their variants, they not only cover all the possibilities of tonal chord progression, but they also reveal its inner logic. They do not define a law, however, but rather encircle an order, with the most commonly-occurring at its center, and with generous space for less frequent solutions on its circumference, with tolerance even for rarities.

How did this order evolve, where did it originate and how did it develop?

When listening to music of the fifteenth or sixteenth century we spontaneously perceive a logic of sound progression. Experience enables us to enjoy the refined compositorial games which are related to creating, fulfilling or deceiving a "hearing expectation". In addition to this, our ears will occasionally recognize a progression which we know from later music. We may, therefore—with good reason—suspect that the logic of sound progression has its history and its own development.

The earliest texts addressing the question of sound progression stem from the beginnings of polyphony. In connection with the descriptions of parallel organum, for example, there are indications concerning the *occursus,* how to lead the voices together at the end of a phrase.[10] The interest in control of intervallic progression increases over the following centuries. Around 1100, the Montpellier treatise suggests an order not only for the beginning and the end, but also for the middle part of a phrase.[11] Perfect consonances, at that time including the fourth, are generally preferred. thirds are allowed; occasional sixths—although still considered dissonant—as well. Some intervals are more suitable for a beginning or an end, others more for middle parts. This is the first known attempt to use the different qualities of the intervals to control the progression of sound. The definitive breakthrough, however, does not occur until the late thirteenth and early fourteenth century. Some intervals are rearranged: the fourth is increasingly considered dissonant, whereas the sixth becomes more acceptable as a consonance.

The new order divides the consonances into two groups, uniting unison, fifth and octave among the perfect, the two thirds and the two sixths among the imperfect ones. Different roles are assigned to these intervals, according to their qualities and their potential. The perfect ones provide stability, and are therefore apt to be used for beginnings and intermediate or final goals. The imperfect ones create instability, and are therefore to be used as instigators of motion. At the Schola Cantorum in Basle we call this the P-i(iii...)-P-principle. One or several imperfect consonances stand

---

10. e.g. Guido of Arezzo as well as Johannes of Afflighem on "diaphony", cf. Claude V. Palisca (ed.), *Hucbald, Guido and John on Music,* translated by Warren Babb, New Haven and London 1978.
11. Hans Heinrich Eggebrecht & Frieder Zaminer, *Ad organum faciendum, Lehrschriften aus nachguidonischer Zeit,* Mainz 1970.

between two perfect ones. The principle is described for the first time by Petrus dictus palma ociosa (Peter who is said to have a lazy hand) in his *Compendium de cantu mensurabili* from 1336. The author explains not only the P-i-P- principle; he also gives a detailed account of the use of Musica Ficta.

An imperfect consonance, led in contrary and stepwise motion to a perfect one, ought to be altered in such a way that one of the voices moves by a minor second. This is to say, one should move to the octave from a major sixth, to the fifth from a major third, and to the unison from a minor third.

Furthermore — and this may be of interest to all who have suffered from this rule — Peter prohibits the parallel motion of two perfect consonances of the same kind. The reason for this is that they make no musical sense, because there is no motion within and none between them.[12]

A melody has a beginning, a path and a goal; it has, in other words, perspective. With the P-i-P-principle a new dimension is added to this. For the first time in music history there is, in addition to the horizontal, also a vertical orientation, with the cadence as one of its most important products.[13] Composers now have a tool at their disposition with which they can plan and steer the sound. This gives the listener a further level of "hearing expectation", and for the composer it opens the doors to an endless and wonderful game. Much more even: The P-i-P-principle is the origin, the prototype so to speak, of all the rules of sound progression; it maintains its universal validity from Machaut to Mahler and is the first and foremost harmonic law for all music based on consonance, notabene also for thoroughbass and for the Rules of the Octave.

Completing two-voice intervallic progressions with one or two other voices leads to two consonant chord structures: The 3-5-8

---

12. These rules apply to the two-voice setting between Cantus and Tenor, in German called *Gerüstsatz*.
13. It may be no coincidence that practically at the same time perspective is introduced and developed in painting.

chord, predominantly marked by the perfect fifth and/or octave, and the 3-6-(8) chord, marked by the imperfect third and sixth. Seen in analogy to the perfect and imperfect intervals, these chords provide the same qualities of stability and instability. And they are, indeed, used in the same fashion. The P-i-P-principle generates the basic order for chord-progression. 3-5-8 chords are used to begin and end, 3-6 chords to create motion in between.

Example 9   a) *perfect + perfect*

b) *perfect + imperfect*

c) *imperfect + perfect and imperfect + imperfect*

Ex.9 is divided into three sections. The original intervals are written with white notes, the possible additions with black notes. Some of the additions exclude one another; the purpose of the graph is to give a synopsis of all the possibilities at once. Fig. a) shows all the options to complement a unison, a fifth and an octave, under the condition that the result will still be perfect. In fig. b) these three intervals are complemented by imperfect consonances. Fig. c) gives all the options to complement a third, a sixth and a tenth. While the chords resulting in the first group practically disappear in the later fifteenth century, the ones in the other two groups only contain the two above-mentioned structures: the 3-5 and the 3-6 chord.

These two structures are, however, results of several different constellations. It is very important not to forget that only two voices form the primary setting and are therefore to be considered the main voices, and that the other(s) fulfill a complementary function and are therefore to be considered subordinate. A 3-5 chord, for example, can be the result of a third in the the main voices completed by a subordinate fifth, or of a fifth in the main voices completed by subordinate third. The result is the same, the meaning is not. There will be more on this hierarchy of voices in due course.

Once the principle of interval progression, the possibilities of combining intervals to form chords, as well as the analogy between intervallic and chord progression are understood, we need more information about what is considered idiomatic in modal harmony. Fortunately there is a great deal of historic information available, from both theory and practice.

Johannes Tinctoris[14] writes about *contrapunctus a mente* and *super librum canere*. Both terms refer to the practice of improvisation on a given melody for two or more voices. This practice is iconographically well-documented in paintings showing musicians behind a table on which there is a book or a vellum with music, often clearly identifiable as a single melodic line. The people sing and play *super librum*, "over the book". Tinctoris leaves no doubt that this practice was intended for several different voices. How was this possible?

Guilielmus Monachus,[15] a contemporary of Tinctoris, shows us how. In his treatise, there is a chapter on the *Contrapunctus Anglicorum,* the counterpoint he attributes to the English, in which he

---

14. Johannes Tinctoris, *Liber de arte contrapuncti,* 1477, edited by Albert Seay in *Johannes Tinctoris Opera Theoretica,* American Institute of Musicology 1965, translated into English and introduced by the same author in *Musicological Studies and Documents,* American Institute of Musicology 1961.

15. Guilielmus Monachus, *De praeceptis artis musicae et practicae compendiosus libellus,* Venice, Bibl. di San Marco, Lat. 336 (Contarini), coll. 1581. Edited by Albert Seay in *Corpus Scriptorum de Musica,* American Institute of Musicology 1965.

explains the practice of polyphonic improvisation.[16] The basis is formed by a two-voice core, consisting of parallels of imperfect consonances, called *gymels*. Parallel thirds, sixths or tenths between perfect consonances at the beginning and at the end do not contradict the P-i-P-principle, they rather represent an extreme case of it. Guilielmus gives examples showing how to add complementary voices. These may in some cases move along in parallels as well, or else counterpoint the pregiven voice with a regular exchange between two intervals. This may sound quite complicated, but in practice it is very simple. Ex. 10 illustrates the most frequently-used four-voice combinations in a graph, with the pregiven voice in the Cantus or in the Tenor marked by a line, and the others relating to them with their intervals, indicated by numbers.

Example 10

   a) Fauxbourdon models:

```
C  ―――――         C   6 6 6 6
A  4 4 4 4       A   3 3 3 3
T  6 6 6 6       T  ―――――
```

   b) other three-voice combinations:

```
Tripl. 4 3 4 3     C  ―――――         C   10 10 10 10
C     ―――――        A   5 6 5 6      A    5  6  5  6
T      3 3 3 3     T   10 10 10 10  T  ―――――
```

   c) the most important four-voice combinations:

```
C  ―――――           C  ―――――         C  ―――――
A   3 3 3 3        A   4 3 4 3      A   5 3 5 3
T   5 6 5 6        T   6 6 6 6      T   5 6 5 6
B  12 10 12 10     B   8 10 8 10    B  10 10 10 10
   ( 5  3  5  3)
```

―――――――――――――

16. cf. Markus Jans, "Alle gegen Eine", in: *Jahrbuch für historische Musikpraxis X,* 1986.

The use of these progression models is indeed quite simple. Problems may occur in connection with cadences and occasionally-resulting diminished fifths. These can easily be resolved by a temporary change of model. The latter may also be used for aesthetic reasons, e.g. for the sake of variety.[17]

Ex. 11 shows beginnings and extracts of pieces from different historic periods, beginning in the early fifteenth and ending in the early eigheenth century. They illustrate the use of improvisation models in compositions, thus documenting the enormous influence these models had on the formation of the harmonic idiom.

Example 11

  a) Gilles Binchois, ed. Wolfgang Rehm, Mainz 1957

  b) Anon., in: Claudio Gallico, Un libro di poesie per musica dell'epoca d'Isabella d'Este, Mantova 1961

---

17. cf. Markus Jans, "Modale Harmonik", in: *Jahrbuch für historische Musikpraxis XVI*, 1992, pp. 171 ff.

(Towards a History of) the Rule of the Octave

c) *Philippe Verdelot, 22 Madrigals, ed. Bernard Thomas, London 1980*

d) *Tomás Luis de Victoria, from the Credo of the Missa quarti toni, ed. Felipe Pedrell, Leipzig 1903, Reprint Ridgewood, New Jersey 1965*

e) *from: Heinrich Schütz, Der Psalter, Neue Ausgabe sämtlicher Werke, Kassel 1955*

f) *from: J. S. Bach, "Heut' ist, o Mensch, ein grosser Trauertag",* 389 Choralgesänge, *ed. Bernhard Friederich Richter, Wiesbaden, Edition Breitkopf Nr. 3765*

In the tenth-parallel model, where the gymel lies between the outer voices, the chord progression includes both 3-5 and 3-6 chords. In the other models the basses are characterized by the typical sequence of fourth-leaps and second-steps. They are responsible for the fact that each and every chord is in "root-position". What about the above-mentioned analogy, then? Where are the unstable chords here? The bass is not the primary counterpoint of the main voice. This role is played by the gymel. The parallel imperfect consonances are the primary sound movers. Secondarily, the regular 12-10-12 respectively 8-10-8 exchange of the bass with the main voice produces a continuous sequence of *perfectiones* or cadences.

Just for fun, one may compare the hierarchic order of the voices to the social system of the middle ages: there are the noble people, called *Bellatores*, and above these, attainable only through scholarship and consecration, is the class of the monks and church clergy, called *Oratores*. Below there are the working class people, called *Laboratores*. The two main voices belong to the upper classes; from the ninth until the fifteenth century these are usually Cantus and Tenor. The complementary voices belong to the working class. Listening to the line of a filler middle voice, one can easily imagine a polite servant doing his job; the leaping basses may recall the picture of a farmer in wooden shoes. This is different for example in the tenth-parallel model: here the bass wears the leather shoes and behaves like a nobleman.

The predetermined distribution of roles begins to disintegrate in the late fifteenth century. Increasingly, each voice can assume any of the tasks and play any of the roles, and they all do this in turn. The primary setting still consists of two voices, however, in constantly changing pairs. Understanding the role of voices in the context of this background is very revealing, also for later music. Composers often use changes of role, particularly in bass lines, to differenciate the (affective) content and to separate parts of the form.

Some of the model combinations shown are clearly associated with music of the Renaissance. Sixteenth-century theory deals with

(Towards a History of) the Rule of the Octave

the subject matter of sound progression either in terms of extended two-voice counterpoint or else in terms of progression models. The two approaches are interrelated, and remain so throughout the centuries to come.

In his instructions on how to improvise instrumental music (1565), Thomas de Sancta Maria[18] extends the number of progression models, and furthermore, he presents them in a systematic order which comes very close to the Rule of the Octave. The main voice, however, to which all the others relate, is still the Cantus. In Vol. II, chapter XI he shows *Ten different ways of ascending stepwise in consonant chords.* Fray Thomas' collection is by far the most complete and probably the most important source for modal sound progression. Ex.12 a) shows an extended model, where the sixth-parallels between Cantus and Tenor are interrupted by a regularly-recurring fifth. The Bass adapts to this pattern and repeatedly changes from fifth to sixth to third. The result is a progression-model of three alternating chords. Ex.12 b) shows the use of contrary motion between Cantus and Bassus. There will be more on this aspect later.

Example 12   a) No. 7

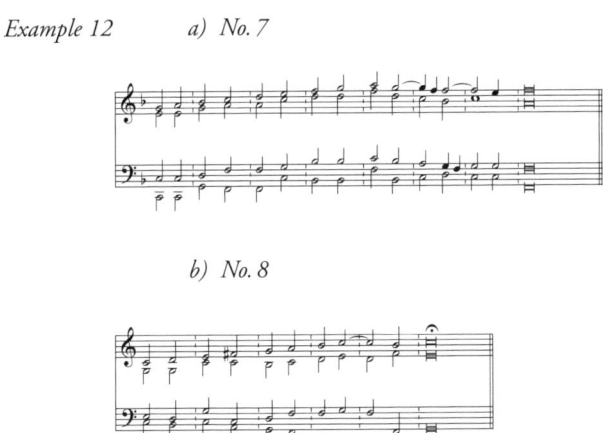

b) No. 8

---

18. Fray Thomas de Sancta Maria, *Libro Llamado El Arte de Taner Fantasia*, Valladolid 1565, translated by Almonte C. Howell and Warren E. Hultberg, in an edition by Yvette E. Miller, Pittsburgh, PA 1991.

I believe that the sixth-parallel (Fauxbourdon) and the tenth-parallel models lead to the harmonic order represented by the Rules of the Octave. The other models maintain a certain validity — their typical sound progressions are still found in the tonal music of the following centuries — but they are no longer as prominent as they were in modal harmony. In order to illustrate this, I would like to examine the tenth-parallel model in somewhat more detail.

According to Guilielmus, the tenth-parallel model may be completed by a free choice of all of the consonant intervals, avoiding two perfect ones of the same kind in a row, however, or else with a regular exchange of fifths and sixths in the middle voice. The latter variant leads to an alternation of 3-5 and 3-6 chords. If started with a 3-5 chord, every third one will be a 3-5 chord again, and therefore apt to function as intermediate or final goal of the sequence. Hence progressions of a third, a fifth or a seventh guarantee a satisfying conclusion. What about progressions of a sixth or a fourth?

The following example is an extract from a madrigal by Philippe Verdelot,[19] entitled *Con lagrime e sospir*. The two added variants are possible model reductions. One of them ends on a 3-6, the other, like Verdelot's, on the desired 3-5 chord.

Example 13   a) Verdelot

---

19. Philippe Verdelot, op. cit. (Ex. 11c)

b) reduction 1

c) reduction 2

Beginning with the b-flat at the end of m.1, the Cantus descends stepwise to the d at the beginning of m. 3. The Bassus accompanies this with parallel tenths. In order to conclude the progression with a 3-5 chord Verdelot employs a trick: he uses the first tenth twice, filling it with a fifth as well as a sixth, thus creating a "double emploi", switching the gears of the model and entering the desired succession of chords. Verdelot's inner voices are not consistent with the model throughout the whole passage. There are a number of probable reasons for these deviations which will not be discussed here.

Does Verdelot conceive a passage like the one in Ex. 13 still thinking in terms of the improvisation models? This question is hard to answer. My guess is that at his time the model-generated sound progressions had become integrated elements of harmonic thinking and conceiving: they had become part of the idiom.

Verdelot's trick of using the same interval twice and filling it differently each time — a "double use" as discussed in connection with Heinichen's practice formula in Ex. 3 — can easily be applied at any other point in the progression.

Example 14   *a)*

b) J. S. Bach

Ex. 14 a) shows the tenth-parallel model used with a descending fourth. Ideally, the two middle chords should both carry the sixth above the Bassus. In so doing, they would, however, produce fifth-parallels with the Cantus. The "double use" on the next-to-last chord avoids these and provides the desired *tendere*. In this example I added another descending fourth to complete the progression, thus leading to one of the Rules of the Octave. Ex. 14 b) shows a well-known application.[20]

Example 15

A different trick is used in Ex. 15. The suspension of a seventh in the next-to-last chord avoids the fifth parallels, and the resolving sixth again provides the desired *tendere*. Here, too, I added another descending fourth to complete the progression. The result is another well-known Rule of the Octave.

At the beginning of his treatise from 1670–71, Johann Nenning,[21] writing under his cloister name Spiridion, gives examples of simple chord progressions which he calls *cadentia*. He shows the student how to improvise elaborations on the keyboard, the ultimate goal being to use these techniques to create greater forms, thus

---

20. J.S.Bach, *O Haupt voll Blut und Wunden*, in: op. cit. (Ex. 11f)
21. Spiridion a Monte Carmelo, *Nova instructio pro pulsandis organis spinettis manuchordis etc.*, Bamberg 1670–71, ed. Edoardo Bellotti, Colledara 2003.

learning how to compose. The following two examples are taken from *cadentia tertia*, using the above-mentioned tricks in sequence.

Example 16   a) Nenning, Cad. III, 7

b) Cad. III, 25

To complete my survey, I should like to come back to the question of contrary motion. A common denominator for all the consonant and most of the dissonant chords is the third above the bass. There are two exceptions, the 4-6 and the 2-4-6 chord, where the third is only suspended and usually follows as a resolution. As a matter of principle therefore, there are third or tenth parallels in every progression. The next example shows two main voices in stepwise and contrary motion through the course of an octave, starting and ending on the fifth degree of C-major. It represents one of the most frequently used models of contrary motion. The bass can easily be supplied with figures according to the octave rule. The written-in extra notes illustrate the above-mentioned tenth parallels working as a basic binding agent.

Example 17

Let us remember Guilielmus's remark that tenth parallels may be filled with any of the consonant intervals, under the condition that parallel perfect ones of the same kind are avoided. If we switch the roles of the voices in Ex. 17 and take the tenth parallels as the primary setting, we can easily understand the top line as a complementary voice in Guilielmus's sense.

The following abstracts show some of the most commonly used contrary-motion models. The numbers represent the degrees with respect to the tonality. The models are organized according to different premises which are given ahead.

Example 18

    a) premise: 1 2 3 to be counterpointed by 3 2 1 and 4 5 6 by 6 5 4

    model:

upper voice ascending: 5 6 7 1 2 3 3 4 5, descending: 5 4 4 3 2 1 7 6 5
lower voice descending: 5 4 4 3 2 1 7 6 5, ascending: 5 6 7 1 2 3 3 4 5

    rule: 3 must be repeated in the ascending, 4 in the descending scale.

    b) premise: 1 2 3 to be counterpointed by 3 2 1 and 5 6 7 by 7 6 5

    model:

upper voice ascending: 5 6 7 7 1 2 3 4 5, descending: 5 4 3 2 1 1 7 6 5
lower voice descending: 7 6 5 4 3 2 1 1 7, descending: 7 7 1 2 3 4 5 6 7

    rule: 7 must be repeated in the ascending, 1 in the descending scale.

The list of models can be extended with changing premises. Some of them work only for parts of the scale and some only for one of the voices and only in one direction, e.g.:

    c) premise: 1 2 3 to be counterpointed by 1 7 6

    model:

upper voice ascending: 1 2 3 4 5 6 6 7 1, descending: 1 7 6 5 4 4 3 2 1
lower voice descending: 1 7 6 6 5 4 3 2 1, ascending: 1 2 2 3 4 5 6 7 1

The given examples do not include all possibilities of stepwise contrary motion, but they give a good account of the most frequently-used ones, in other words the most idiomatic ones.

I have now reached the end of my exposé. Aware of its rather rhapsodic character, I hope, all the same, to have succeeded in illustrating the most important aspects of the historic development of the Rule of the Octave. Its history plays a prominent role in the development of harmonic tonality. The "story" can be told in greater detail and with more continuity. It is my intention to come back to it in a different format in due course.[22]

---

22. My heartfelt thanks go to my wife, Sally Jans-Thorpe, for her patient help in translating this paper into English.

THOROUGHBASS AS A PATH TO COMPOSITION IN THE EARLY EIGHTEENTH CENTURY

Joel Lester

During the past generation, the history of music theory has drawn an unprecedented degree of scholarly attention, culminating in two separate multi-authored histories.[1] We have developed a tremendous amount of what might best be referred to as journalistic knowledge concerning the ways that musicians of earlier periods thought about musical structures—journalistic in the sense of reporting what they wrote and the context within which they wrote. (It is astonishing how recent our relatively comprehensive knowledge of that information is. As one indication, consider the availability of reprints of major treatises from the past. Rameau's *Traité de l'harmonie*, the foundation of modern notions of harmonic theory, was not available other than in its original edition until 1967, when two facsimile editions appeared.[2] For the preceding two and a half centuries, the work existed solely in its original Paris 1722 edition.)

Now that we have that knowledge, what might we do with it? One option is to explore with hitherto unsurpassed confidence how musicians of past eras conceptualized the process by which they composed. In this paper, I consider what we might be able to understand about harmony and voice-leading as used in the music of J. S. Bach's time without invoking the modern analytic tools that were developed either late in Bach's lifetime, or, in most cases, well after his death. What sorts of sense did contemporaneous concepts and tools, as opposed to later concepts and tools, make? By harmony and voice-leading I mean not only the chords

---

1. Frieder Zaminer (ed.), *Geschichte der Musiktheorie*, 11 vols., Darmstadt 1984-, and Thomas Christensen (ed.), *The Cambridge History of Western Music Theory*, Cambridge 1999.
2. New York, and in volume 1 of Erwin Jacobi (ed.), *The Complete Theoretical Writings of Jean-Philippe Rameau*, s.l.

themselves and their connections, but also their placement and roles within compositions.

By raising these questions, I proceed from the premise that musicians understood what they were doing, or—to put it another way—that musicians did not have to await posthumous theories and the posthumous development of analytical tools in order to understand what it was they had been doing. I do not reject later perspectives (analytic concepts, methods, and tools). I know full well that later perspectives on music from all eras have revealed aspects of that music that might well have not been consciously articulated by the musicians of the given time. Nor do I reject the questions about musical structure raised by later perspectives—indeed, I frequently am asking those very questions based on later theoretical perspectives, even when I use early eighteenth-century notions to help me answer those questions. I also understand and accept that musicians of a given era often groped in the dark until (frequently posthumous) developments shed light on some aspects of their activities or raised the questions that those earlier musicians could not, would not, or did not frame "properly" (according to modern conceptions). But I also argue that musicians of any given era probably did not know that they were groping for answers to questions that would not be framed until the next generation.

I first summarize some salient aspects of thoroughbass and provide instances which I believe demonstrate that one can say a great deal about harmony and voice-leading in the music of Bach's generation without invoking later harmonic theories and concerns. At the end of this paper, I raise a number of questions about what I have accomplished.

Thoroughbass in the late seventeenth and early eighteenth centuries was much more than the vestiges that remain in harmonic theory nowadays—vestiges that consist primarily of using Arabic numerals to indicate chord inversions or to signal the addition of nonharmonic tones to chords. In those earlier centuries, thoroughbass was the way that musicians thought about harmony and voice-leading. I stress the word "musicians" here, for thoroughbass was not only for accompanists. Rather, the discipline of thoroughbass comprised a way of conceptualizing a range of musical structures for all musicians. In particular for our purposes here, it was the path through which composers learned the grammar of harmony—how to construct verticalities of all sorts (the basic chords as well as a host of elaborations of those chords), how to connect them to make a wide range of sensible progressions, how to elaborate and vary those progressions, and how and where to place those elaborated progressions in musical improvisations and compositions.

A very brief history.[3] Thoroughbass apparently arose in the late sixteenth century as a way of filling in the parts in multi-part music when there were too few players around (probably originally in domestic performances). At first, just the continuous bass notes were written out. Not long after that, numbers and other symbols (accidentals, horizontal and diagonal lines, and so forth) were used to indicate the intervals over the bass, especially at points where 5/3 chords that agreed with the key signature were not appropriate. (Thoroughbass was far from the sole shorthand developed around this time for the purpose of facilitating performances and accompaniments when a full ensemble was not present. In Spain, for instance, where the guitar was popular as an accompanying instrument, *alfabeto* notation—letters of the alphabet indicating various finger-placements on the fingerboard—arose around the same time, namely in the late sixteenth century.[4])

During the seventeenth and eighteenth centuries, thoroughbass became the shorthand for all sorts of compositional and performance issues. I will focus here on two of these: how thoroughbass dealt with unfigured basses, and thoroughbass as a path to composition.

Thoroughbass arose, of course, primarily as an abbreviated notation for accompanists. Therefore, when thoroughbass notations

---

3. In English, the most comprehensive history of the development of thoroughbass remains the opening chapters of Frank Thomas Arnold, *The Art of Accompaniment from a Thoroughbass*, London 1931 and New York 1965.
4. Thomas Christensen discusses *alfabeto* notation in "The Spanish Baroque Guitar and Seventeenth-Century Triadic Theory", in: *Journal of Music Theory* 36 (1992), pp. 1–42.

were absent, one of its main functions could not be fulfilled. During nearly two centuries, writers of thoroughbass treatises frequently complained that unfigured basses made it impossible for an accompanist to know which chords to play. But the fact that these complaints appeared in print generation after generation proves that the problem of unfigured basses never disappeared. We in the twenty-first century should be thankful that sloth—a seemingly unchanging aspect of human nature—led those who wrote thoroughbasses to omit figures. Because unfigured basses were ubiquitous, many of those who wrote thoroughbass manuals for professional musicians (and for advanced amateurs) believed that they had to explain standard compositional patterns—common paradigms of harmonies and voice-leading. Due to their explanations, thoroughbass evolved into a general framework for thinking about harmony and voice-leading, and, from there, into a pathway leading to composition.

There were two main routes from thoroughbass to composition: via improvising on thoroughbass patterns, and via ornamenting thoroughbass patterns until the results resembled compositions. In order to present either path, thoroughbass instruction began by presenting harmonies and their connection via voice-leading. The harmonies presented were not only the triads and seventh chords that musicians ever since Rameau have routinely considered the basic harmonies, but all verticalities that might occur at the beginning of bass notes (what we now call suspensions and appoggiaturas added to harmonies, accented passing tones, and the like). If thoroughbass instruction was to lead to composition, just knowing harmonies and voice leading was insufficient. A composer also had to know how to create sensible structures within which these harmonies and voice leadings would appear. Musicians knew from experience that not every possible verticality could sensibly follow any other possible verticality. How could one explain which verticalities made sense? Or, if one could not explain what made sense and why desirable progressions made sense, it was at least necessary to impart guidance to avoid those successions that were problematic.

Discussions of unfigured basses, a topic that did not appear in all thoroughbass treatises, inevitably led to a consideration of compositional norms in terms of harmonies and voice-leading. Starting early in the seventeenth century, musicians realized that when the bass had specific patterns, the harmonies that appeared tended to be formulaic. There were several ways of finding such formulas. Some early writers pointed to a specific solmization syllable, usually *mi*, the lower note of a semitone. Remember that six-syllable (or hexachordal) solmization with mutation was still the norm.[5] *Mi* in the bass would carry a 6/3 chord; even when *mi* did not lead directly to *fa*. Michael Praetorius (c. 1569–1621) presented this notion in 1619.[6] This rule, when applied to the diatonic notes of a major key, ensured that what we call I^6 appeared instead of root-position III over scale-step 3, and that V^6 routinely appeared instead of root-position VII over scale-step 7. But in minor keys, the rule did not work as well — it was effective in ensuring a proper harmony over scale-steps 2 and raised scale-step 7, but was not at all applicable to scale-step 5 (which merited what we call the dominant triad, not a 6/3 chord).

This rule (and others like it) became increasingly inadequate as the harmonic language of the time became more complex during the seventeenth century. In a slightly more sophisticated method, writers pointed to notational symbols that might suggest a proper chord. One such rule, appearing in numerous thoroughbass treatises, instructed that a bass note with a sharp should carry a 6/3 chord. This would work for ensuring a proper chord over the leading tone in minor keys, and also for ensuring a proper chord when

---

5. As late as the 1710s, the relative value of six-syllable solmization with mutation versus seven-syllable solmization was still hotly disputed, and six-syllable solmization with mutation remained common in discussions of contemporaneous music at least through the end of the eighteenth century. One of the two primary topics in a ferocious letter exchange from 1717–18 between Johann Joseph Fux and Johann Mattheson was solmization. Mattheson published the letter exchange (and all the other letters he received from other musicians on these topics) in *Criticae musicae*, Hamburg 1725, pp. 179–288. An English translation by the current author appears in "The Fux-Mattheson Correspondence: An Annotated Translation", in: *Current Musicology* 23 (1977), pp. 37–62. On the very first page of his *Gründliche Anweisung zur Composition*, Leipzig 1790, Johann Albrechtsberger still used six-syllable solmization in his presentation of the major and minor scales.
6. Michael Praetorius, *Syntagma Musicum*, vol. 3, Wolfenbüttel 1619, p. 134. Reprinted by Eduard Bernoulli (ed.), Leipzig 1906, p. 106.

what we call a secondary dominant was to be used over a chromatic leading tone in the bass. But the rule was not at all applicable in keys with many sharps in the signature (such as F# minor). As more and more keys came to be commonly used, such rules became unusable.

In an attempt to discover more reliable indicators of the proper harmony, writers later in the seventeenth century began to note that various bass motions, measured by the intervals involved, would frequently carry the same specific harmonies. For instance, a bass note lying a third above the bass of a preceding or subsequent 5/3 chord usually had a 6/3 chord (leading to what we now call the progressions I–I⁶ and I⁶–I, V–V⁶ and V⁶–V, and so forth), as shown in Ex. 1a. There were similar recommendations for other bass motions involving two notes.

Example 1. Some common thoroughbass patterns
a) Basses rising or falling a third, with the lower note having a 5/3 chord.
b) I–vii⁶–I⁶
c) I–vii⁶–I⁶, vii⁶–I⁶–V⁴/², I⁶–ii⁶–V

Other bass patterns were longer than two notes. For instance, three ascending notes in a row after a 5/3 chord would often have the sequence of harmonies 5/3–#6/3–6/3 (that is, I–vii⁶–I⁶ in modern notation), as shown in Ex. 1b. Such patterns were useful to a point. But if there were too many of them, how could a musician remember them all? Such discussions grew to immense size in treatises that tried to be comprehensive, such as the popular treatise by the Italian Lorenzo Penna (1613–1693).[7] Ultimately, there

---

[7]. Penna's *Li primi albori musicali* first appeared in Bologna in 1672, and was reprinted there in 1679, 1684, 1696. Another edition appeared in Antwerp in 1690. The 1684 edition appears in facsimile, Bologna 1969. Treatises from a bit later by Saint Lambert and Francesco Gasparini have similarly extensive discussions of bass patterns. Saint Lambert, *Les principes du clavecin*, Paris 1702, facsimile edition, Geneva 1974, English

were too many rules and exceptions to make pedagogical sense. This problem was compounded by the growing number of verticalities in common use. In the mid 1600s, comprehensive thoroughbass treatises might list thirty or forty possible thoroughbass figurings; by the early 1700s, some treatises listed over a hundred. In addition, it became clear that the rules were often applicable only in limited circumstances. For instance, if the bass pattern in Ex. 1b (three rising notes) were repeated on successively higher scale degrees, different harmonies would have to be used, as shown in Ex. 1c.

Around 1700, many writers began to look to scale-step placement to explain what harmony might appear over a given bass note. They did this primarily by presenting scale fragments. In 1716, the French guitarist François Campion (c. 1686–1748) combined these scale fragments into a complete octave and named it the Rule of the Octave (shown here in Ex. 2).[8] Even though

Example 2. The Rule of the Octave, as presented in Campion, 1716

Campion presented the Rule of the Octave in print for the first time. The Rule surely existed in one form or another before 1716, and Campion himself did not take credit for inventing it.

---

translation by Rebecca Harris-Warwick as *'Principles of the Harpsichord' by Monsieur de Saint Lambert*, Cambridge 1984. Gasparini, *L'armonico practico al cimbalo*, Venice 1708, later editions through 1802 (!), facsimile edition, New York 1967, English translation by Frank Stillings as *The Practical Harmonist at the Harpsichord*, New Haven 1968.

8. *Traité d'accompagnement et de composition, selon la regle des octaves*, Paris 1716, facsimile edition, Geneva 1976, English translation by Luann Dragone in "François Campion's Treatise on Accompaniment: A Translation and Commentary", in: *Theoria* 6 (1992), pp. 135–162.

Campion explained that the Rule of the Octave was to be practiced in every major and minor key—he actually wrote out the figured bass in all those keys, offering one of the earlier presentations of all 24.[9] The Rule solved many of the issues problematic in the work of earlier thoroughbass writers. The use of chords in the Rule was tied to scale steps—no longer did it matter what the solmization syllable was, what the bass pattern was, or whether there were sharps or flats in the key signature. For instance, consider the progression in Ex. 1c. All the harmonies there are indicated in the Rule, either in its ascending or descending form. The first five harmonies (appearing in mm. 1 and 2) are the indicated chords in the ascending Rule of the Octave. (The third chord is the same in both the ascending and descending form of the Rule.) The next harmony (the 4/2 chord at the end of m. 2) is the appropriate chord for descending into the following 6/3 chord, as in the descending Rule of the Octave. The harmonies in the third measure are those of the ascending Rule of the Octave. And the final two harmonies are a standard cadence.

The biggest problem with the Rule of the Octave is that although it works reasonably well with scale fragments, it often fails to indicate the proper chord for basses containing skips. Scale-step 2, for instance, often supported what we call vii^6 or V$^{4/3}$ when the bass moved by step to scale-steps 1 or 3. But when the bass moved from scale-step 2 to scale-step 5, the common harmony over scale-step 2 was often what we call ii (a chord not indicated in the Rule).

As a result, even treatises that relied heavily on the Rule of the Octave also introduced other patterns as well in order to present patterns or chords that were appropriate to specific places within a piece or section of a piece. These include tonic pedals and closely

---

9. The first publication listing all 24 keys is apparently Jacques Ozanam, *Dictionaire mathematique*, Amsterdam 1691, p. 660—strikingly, a mathematical, not a musical work. The earliest musical publications to list all 24 keys were Thomas Balthasar Janowka, *Clavis ad thesaurum magnae artis musicae*, Prague 1701, partial English translation in Joel Lester, *Between Modes and Keys: German Theory 1592–1802*, Stuyvesant 1989; Sébastien de Brossard, *Dictionaire de musique*, Paris 1703; Alexandre Frère, *Transpositions de musique*, Paris 1706; and Johann David Heinichen, *Neu erfundene und gründliche Anweisung … des General-Basses*, Hamburg 1711.

Thoroughbass as a Path to Composition

Example 3. *Two progressions suggested for tonic pedals by C. P. E. Bach, 1762, chapter 41 (chapter 7 in the English translation)*

related progressions that occur at beginnings and endings of pieces (or large sections of pieces), some of which appear in Ex. 3; dominant pedals that would appear before a concluding passage, as shown in Ex. 4; and various sorts of cadential progressions and voice-leadings.

Example 4. *Two progressions suggested for dominant pedals by C. P. E. Bach, 1762, ibid)*

In the hands of accomplished musicians, a combination of the norms of the Rule of the Octave with other insights could yield quite sophisticated recommendations for placing harmonic progressions within a passage of a composition, even without a "theory of harmonic progressions" — something that did not exist prior to Rameau. One of the most imaginative theorists of the time was Johann David Heinichen (1683–1729). In his treatises of both 1711 and 1728, he discussed unfigured basses extensively.[10] He not only included abstract discussions (rules of various sorts), but also illustrated the application of his procedures by filling in the harmonies in an extant piece of music.

---

10. *Neu erfundene Anweisung*, 1711, and *Der General-Bass in der Composition*, Dresden 1728.

Example 5. A recitative by A. Scarlatti, unfigured bass realized in Heinichen, 1728

His most extensive such demonstration is of an entire cantata by Alessandro Scarlatti. Ex. 5 offers the beginning of a recitative from that cantata. Heinichen explains that "An experienced accompanist" would recognize that "this progression forms a half cadence ... even though the half cadence is broken off after the A\6+, and in place of the final G an unrelated F#\b7 chord is taken; this latter chord is only an inversion of the preceding A\6# whose resolution to G follows".[11] In this remarkable sentence, Heinichen makes it clear that he understands a progression of five harmonies over four measures as a single harmonic motion (a half cadence), that the progression's harmonies are based on a norm that a musician would recognize (namely, the descending portion of the Rule of the Octave through scale-steps 8-7-6-5), and that the progression could be interrupted by a variant of one of the harmonies (what he calls an "inversion", but actually a more complex relation than that because the "inverted" chord adds an E-flat not present in the preceding harmony).

Heinichen was for many years the thoroughbass player at the Dresden opera. His discussion clearly gives us a glimpse into the thinking of adept musicians and how they conceptualized harmonic progressions in the era before there existed modern harmonic theories based on root motions and abstract relations of chords to a key center. Without any modern harmonic theory that musicians of the past 250 years have taken for granted, Heinichen

---

11. An English translation of Heinichen's entire discussion appears in George Buelow, "Heinichen's Treatment of Dissonance", in: *Journal of Music Theory* 6 (1962), pp. 216–74, reprinted in George Buelow, *Thorough-bass Accompaniment According to Johann David Heinichen*, Ann Arbor ²1986.

demonstrates a conscious knowledge of how the Rule of the Octave, combined with notions of thoroughbass (or contrapuntal) elaboration and the rhetoric of musical phrases (where a progression belongs in a section of a composition), can unerringly lead to the creation of appropriate harmonic progressions.

The primary path from sophisticated usage of thoroughbass to composition lay in improvisation. Carl Philipp Emanuel Bach, at the end of his 1762 thoroughbass treatise, explains how to improvise—a discussion most probably strongly influenced by the teachings of his father.[12] After a general discussion of extempore playing, C. P. E. Bach turns to the creation of a prelude. "The bass should play the ascending and descending scale of the prescribed key with a variety of thoroughbass signatures and perform the resultant progressions arpeggiated or chordally. A tonic pedal point is convenient for establishing the tonality at the beginning and end. A dominant pedal point can also be introduced effectively before the end". C. P. E. Bach illustrates numerous options for the "variety of thoroughbass signatures" in ascending and descending scales, as well as a few options for tonic and dominant pedal points. The very first scale that he illustrates is the Rule of the Octave (although he does not label it as such). The later scales carry more complex thoroughbass figures, many of these with two or more harmonies on a single bass note elaborating the underlying the chords of the Rule of the Octave.

In fact, the prelude structure that C. P. E. Bach describes agrees quite closely with the structure of the C-major Prelude from the first volume of his father's *The Well-Tempered Clavier*, as shown on the first staff of Ex. 6. As I have described elsewhere, there is a tonic "frame" (a looser term than "pedal" that I use to denote both actual tonic pedals and also key-defining progressions, usually tonic-predominant-dominant-tonic), a descending bass scale through an octave with harmonies elaborating the chords from the

---

12. *Versuch über die wahre Art das Clavier zu spielen*, Part 2, Berlin 1762, chapter 41, English translation by William Mitchell under the title *Essay on the True Art of Playing Keyboard Instruments*, New York 1949, chapter 7 (Mitchell combines many brief chapters from the original edition into much longer chapters).

Example 6. J.S. Bach, Four Preludes from the The Well-Tempered Clavier, 1: C major, C minor, D major, E minor. The underlying thoroughbasses.

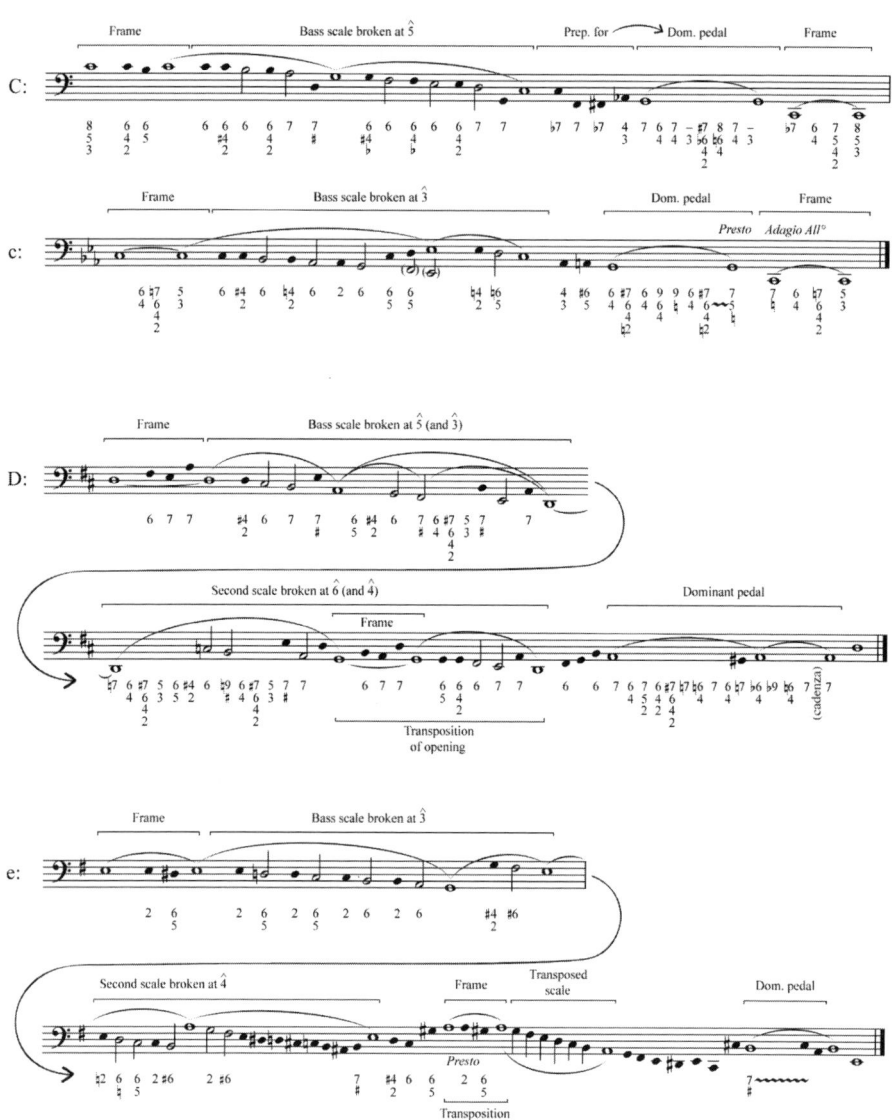

Thoroughbass as a Path to Composition

Rule of the Octave, a dominant pedal preceded by a preparatory progression, and a tonic pedal.[13] C. P. E. Bach's description also pertains to several other preludes in the same collection by his father, including those in c minor, d major, and e minor, as shown by the remainder of Ex. 6.

It is highly likely that J. S. Bach explained the structures of these preludes to his son pretty much in the form that C. P. E. described them in print a dozen years after his father's death. After all, earlier forms of these preludes first appeared in the *Clavierbüchlein vor Wilhelm Friedemann Bach*, a pedagogical collection that J. S. Bach put together for C. P. E. Bach's older brother a couple of years before J. S. completed the manuscript for the entire *Well-Tempered Clavier*.[14]

As Ex. 6 demonstrates, each of these four preludes follows the same order of events as that in C major, with various differences. For instance, the Prelude in C minor, which begins its bass scale with some harmonies identical to those in the C-major Prelude (with adjustment to the minor mode), breaks its octave scale at scale-step 3 (not scale-step 5, as in the C-major Prelude), uses more variants of its arpeggiation pattern, and includes a variety of tempos (especially during its dominant and tonic pedals). Quite interesting is the recomposition of the closing tonic frame in a wholly different texture (a texture whose chords and melismas are reminiscent of the opening movements of the G-minor and A-minor Sonatas for Solo Violin, movements that are also preludes to fugues, and that also begin with tonic frames followed by descending bass scales).[15]

The two other preludes from the first volume of *The Well-Tempered Clavier* in Ex. 6 show a variety of additional traits typical of music of Bach's time. In the D-major Prelude, for instance,

---

13. My more extensive discussion of this prelude from *The Well-Tempered Clavier* and three related preludes from that volume appears in "Bach Teaches Us How to Compose: Four Pattern Preludes from *The Well-Tempered Clavier*", in: *College Music Society Symposium* 38 (1998), pp. 33–46.
14. The *Clavierbüchlein* appears in a facsimile edition, New Haven 1959.
15. I discuss these movements more extensively in *Bach's Works for Solo Violin: Style, Structure, Performance*, New York 1999, chapter 2.

the opening frame presents the same harmonies as in the C-major Prelude, but with the bass of each harmony presenting their "fundamental basses" (Rameauian theory's name for the chordal roots). In both the D-major and E-minor preludes, there are two scalar descents through an octave — the first close in harmonies to those in the C-major and C-minor preludes, respectively; the second emphasizing different harmonies, namely the subdominant side of the key.

Each of these latter two preludes (in D major and E minor) also hint at the structures of larger and more complex movements. In the D-major Prelude, for instance, the opening tonic frame recurs literally transposed midway through the second bass scale, as if it were a ritornello. In the E-minor Prelude, the opening tonic frame recurs at the beginning of the *Presto*, hinting at a technique in some partitas, where the openings of the various dance movements utilize the same progressions, or in which the beginning of a prelude and the beginning of the following fugue are related to one another by the underlying thoroughbass. (For instance, the implicit underlying thoroughbasses of the various movements of the Partita No. 2 in D minor for Solo Violin are closely related to one another, and a progression near the opening of the *Adagio* from the Sonata No.1 in G minor for Solo Violin recurs literally near the opening of the following *Fuga*.[16])

I believe that an accomplished early eighteenth-century musician would have swiftly recognized these demonstrations of compositional possibilities for what they are. Remember Heinichen's remark about what an "experienced accompanist" would recognize — Heinichen's assumption involved a much more sophisticated matter of musical structure than that discussed here. Remember too that the notion of a "musical artwork" did not yet exist in the aesthetics of music. J. S. Bach's purpose in collections like *The Well-Tempered Clavier*, the Inventions, the solo-violin pieces, the *Clavierbüchlein*, and so forth, was clearly to demonstrate how to compose a piece by composing a model piece. The title page of the

---

16. Concerning the movements of the Partita No. 2 in D minor, see *Bach's Works for Solo Violin*, pp. 143–147. Concerning the cited relationship in the Sonata No. 1 in G minor, see *Bach's Works for Solo Violin*, pp. 72–73.

Example 7. J. S. Bach, Sonata No.1 in G minor for Solo Violin, Adagio, with underlying thoroughbass

Inventions explicitly states that the pieces exemplify "good *inventiones*" (or musical ideas) and how to "develop them well".[17]

This quick survey of some principles of thoroughbass and their application by J. S. Bach in a few exemplary compositions shows how composers of the early eighteenth century, in the absence of any theory of harmonic directionality and function (in the senses that we understand those terms since Rameau), could learn to utilize common progressions appropriate to different sections of a composition, could tailor those progressions to the individual circumstances of a given composition, and could create the traits of various compositional circumstances (such as ritornellos).

---

17. The title page of the Inventions appears in many editions. An English translation appears in Hans David and Arthur Mendel, *The Bach Reader*, New York 1945, revised ed., New York 1966, p. 86.

How far can we extend this perspective? For instance, where else in Bach's can we find such patterns? Consider the thoroughbass underlying the opening section of the *Adagio* from the Sonata No. 1 in G-minor for Solo Violin in Ex. 7. This is a more complex movement than the pattern-preludes from *The Well-Tempered Clavier* described above, with a complex web of motivic relationships, with a more complex overall structure to the movement as a whole that includes a change of key before the first cadence in m. 9, and a texture that focuses the listener's attention more on the melismatic melodies than on the underlying bass. But the underlying thoroughbass is quite similar. There is still a tonic frame (with scale-steps 1-2-5-1 in the bass, as in the frame that opens the Prelude in D major from *The Well-Tempered Clavier*, though the chord over scale-step 2 is #6/3 in the G-minor *Adagio* and not 7/5/3, as in the D-major Prelude), followed by more mobile progressions (in essence, a pair of descending scales in the bass), and an elaborated cadence. Numerous other Bach movements have comparable underlying structures.

The extent to which these generic thoroughbass progressions can be tailored to the individual circumstances of a given piece is obvious from comparing the opening of the C-major Prelude from the first volume of *The Well-Tempered Clavier* with two quite different compositions that begin with the very same thoroughbass figuring. Ex. 8 shows the openings of this C-major Prelude,

Example 8.
a) J. S. Bach, Prelude in C Major, The Well-Tempered Clavier, 1, mm. 1-4

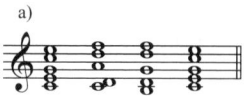

b) J. S. Bach, Partita No. 2 for Solo Violin, Chaconne, opening

c) J. S. Bach, Cantata No. 4 ("Christ lag in Todesbanden"), opening

the Chaconne from the Partita No. 2 for Solo Violin, and the Sinfonia from Cantata No. 4 ("Christ lag in Todesbanden"). Each offers a different texture, a different number of voices, different implicit tempos (since none of these movements carries an explicit tempo marking), and a different melodic line related to the traits of the ensuing piece.

In the C-major Prelude, the melodic line proceeds with scale-steps 3-4-5. That structure supports the entire prelude: an octave descent of the tonic chord under scale-step 3 (in mm. 1-19), a dominant-seventh pedal ending with the seventh (scale-step 4) in the melody, and an arrival on the closing tonic pedal with scale-step 3 in the melody. The same motion among scale steps 3-4-3 also hints at the subject of the fugue that follows, in that the fugue subject begins with a motion up to scale-step 3 and then a 3-4-3 neighbor pattern. (Indeed, the melody of mm. 1-8 in the prelude outlines most of the fugue subject: *E-F-E-A-D-G*-[C] in the prelude and [C-D-]*E-F-E-A-D-G* opening the fugue subject.)

The same thoroughbass progression used as the opening tonic frame of the Chaconne supports a different melodic structure (moving up to scale-step 3 at the end of the progression, instead of beginning with scale-step 3), and emphasizes a different set of motives. In particular, the repeated notes (both within harmonies, such as the melodic A's in m. 1, and across harmonies, such as the E's in m. 2) play prominent roles during various groupings of the ensuing variations (in the chordal section early in the D-major music, and again later in the D-major music when repeated pairs of sixteenths, then three-note groups of sixteenths emerge to dominate the texture).

Example 9.

  a) J. S. Bach, Prelude in D major, The Well-Tempered Clavier, 2, opening

  b) J. S. Bach, Prelude in C major, The Well-Tempered Clavier, 1, opening

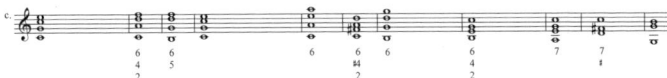

In the Sinfonia to "Christ lag in Todesbanden", Bach brings to the fore yet another possibility inherent in this progression when it occurs in the minor mode — here, Bach stresses the numerous semitones that arise in the voice-leading in order to depict the mournful affect of the text. The chorale melody that Bach inherited begins with an anguishing semitone from scale-step 5 to that scale step's leading tone (scale-step #4 in the overall key) that agonizingly wrenches the opening phrase of the chorale into the dominant key after its very first note. The pervasive semitones in the quasi-imitative orchestral texture stress a voice-leading potential within this thoroughbass progression that is not particularly evident in the other two pieces studied here.

In fact, relatively few thoroughbass patterns commonly appear for given compositional purposes, which is why different pieces by Bach frequently feature identical or nearly identical underlying thoroughbass figurings in analogous structural locations. For instance, a particularly striking recurrence of a portion of the descending octave scale from the C-major Prelude appears in the D-major Prelude from the second volume of *The Well-Tempered Clavier*, as shown in Ex. 9. It is hard to think of two preludes from *The Well-Tempered Clavier* that are more different from one another. The C-major Prelude is, as discussed above, in effect a written-out thoroughbass progression, with a single arpeggiation pattern enlivening all the chords that progress from one to another at the same pace throughout almost the entire piece. The D-major Prelude from the second volume is one of those late pieces of Bach's that imitate the newer styles of the 1740s. It opens with two very contrasting (and *galant*!) thematic ideas in the very opening phrase: a "Mannheim rocket theme" featuring a rising arpeggio, followed by a sighing figure — both in a completely homophonic texture. And the D-major Prelude in the large is cast in a proto-sonata-form, with a repeated "exposition" that modulates from the tonic to dominant, an extended "development", and a complete recapitulation. Yet … for the passage that leaves the tonic key in both these preludes (in C major from volume 1 and D major from volume 2), Bach used the identical underlying thoroughbass — a portion of a descending bass octave (scale steps 8-7-6-5) with identical harmonies.

In the creative imagination of a superb composer like J. S. Bach, familiarity with these ubiquitous and immensely malleable thoroughbass patterns and knowledge of their appropriate placement within a piece allowed for the greatest variety of compositional opportunities. Consider the C-minor Fugue from the first volume of *The Well-Tempered Clavier* and some aspects of its underlying thoroughbass in comparison to the parallel aspects of the underlying thoroughbass structure in the C-minor Prelude. As noted above, the underlying thoroughbass of the fugue subject is a variant of the thoroughbass underlying the tonal frame that opens the prelude. Exx. 10a and 10b juxtapose the two thoroughbasses.

Motivic similarities (especially the many neighbor notes) reinforce the relationship between these two passages. When the fugue ends with the subject appearing with a chordal accompaniment over a literal tonic pedal (as at the opening of the prelude), this implicit relationship between the opening of the prelude and the opening of the fugue becomes more explicit. In addition, the

Example 10.
a) J. S. Bach, Prelude in C minor, The Well-Tempered Clavier, 1, the opening tonal frame expressed as a thoroughbass

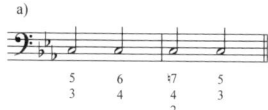

b) J. S. Bach, Fugue in C minor, The Well-Tempered Clavier, 1, the fugue subject and its underlying thoroughbass

c) J. S. Bach, Fugue in C minor, The Well-Tempered Clavier, 1, the episode in mm. 22-24, with a new motive appearing in m. 24

Picardy third that ends the fugue also recalls the return of the prelude's opening tonic frame at the end. In the prelude, this recurrence also emphasizes the major tonic triad and also occurs over a tonic pedal.

Knowing these relationships between this prelude and fugue suggests that other passages in the fugue likewise relate to the prelude. One of the characteristics of the C-minor Fugue is a seemingly almost obsessive preoccupation with the opening motive of the fugue subject. The sixteenth-note neighbor figure that opens the subject occurs not only during the subject (three times, no less, at the same pitch level), but also is the basis of the imitation in many of the episodes. (In addition, Bach found opportunities to introduce that opening motive in other locations, such as in the middle voice immediately before the entry of the bass in the fugal exposition, as if the performer had made a metric mistake and had begun the third entry of the exposition a beat too soon.) And since the fugue offers several statements of the subject and a recurrence of almost every episode, that opening motive appears almost everywhere. A notable exception to that pervasive motive occurs in the return of the descending circle-of-fifths episode. The modulating episode in mm. 9-10 (an episode that leads the music to E-flat major for an appearance of the subject and its two countersubjects in mm. 11-12) recurs beginning in m. 22. But this time, the circle of fifths remains in the key of C minor, and as the episode is extended to allow for the full circle-of-fifths progression, the motive disappears and a new figure appears in its place in m. 24, as Ex. 10c shows. A listener might believe that Bach finally realized he had been presenting this motive too often and broke into a new pattern for variety's sake. But the pattern that Bach introduces is, of course, closely related to the neighboring figure of the prelude. If this were an isolated relationship, there would seem to be little point to invoking such a connection. But in the context of the other interactions between the thoroughbass underlying both this prelude and this fugue, it is a moment of compositional rhapsody of the highest order.

The pattern that C. P. E. Bach recommends as the basis of a prelude is also the common underlying structure of a ritornello: establish the tonic, present a mobile progression (a sequence, more rapid harmonic motion with more varied harmonies than a tonic "frame", and so forth), and move to a cadence. A full discussion of this issue would far exceed the scope of the present study—but I include it to suggest that the fundamentals of thoroughbass progressions that were practiced routinely by musicians of the early eighteenth century would give "an experienced accompanist" (to cite once again Heinichen's phrase) all the information necessary to compose the largest-scale compositions of that era.

Of course progressions by themselves—even elaborated progressions that presented the chords in fancy arpeggiations (as C. P. E. Bach suggested)—would not give rise by itself to the varied surface textures of music of the time. Composers learned to create those surfaces through variations. Friedrich Erhard Niedt's *Musicalische Handleitung* offers the most extensive discussion explaining how to do just that.[18] After teaching how to realize a

---

18. The *Musicalische Handleitung* appeared in three parts, with the first two of those appearing in two editions: Part 1 in 1700 and 1710; Part 2 in 1706 and 1721; Part 3 in 1717. Both reprints and the third part appeared posthumously, with the composer and theorist Johann Mattheson editing the later editions. An English translation by Pamela Poulin and Irmgard Taylor appears in *The Musical Guide*, Oxford 1988.

thoroughbass in the traditional manner in his first volume, Niedt turns in the second volume to teach how to elaborate a thoroughbass to turn it into a composition. First, he shows how to embellish intervals. Then Niedt shows how to use these elaborations to create pieces. He composes an eleven-movement suite based on variants of a single thoroughbass. The suite begins with a toccata (in effect, a written-out improvisation on that same thoroughbass) and ends with a chaconne (also based on the underlying thoroughbass). Several movement openings appear in Ex. 11. The

Example 11. Niedt, Musicalische Handleitung, Part 2. The beginnings of several suite movements built as a single thoroughbass

result is a suite not all that different in conception from J. S. Bach's Partita No. 2 in D minor for Solo Violin, in which there are deep connections among the thoroughbasses of the individual movements, shown in Ex. 12, and where the final movement is a chaconne whose theme has a thoroughbass related to the openings of other movements. Remember that the original meaning of the term "partita" was a set of variations or "little divisions", a title that Bach continued to use occasionally, as in his *Partite diverse* BWV 766-768. (To be sure, many other suites and partitas by Bach and

Example 12. J. S. Bach, Partita No. 2 in D minor for Violin Solo. The thoroughbass progressions underlying the beginnings of all the movements

others do not feature such close relationships between their movements, since the term *partita* was also used as a synonym for *suite*.)

I believe the approach outlined here makes it credible that Bach and his contemporaries might have thought about harmony and voice leading in sophisticated ways, and might have known how to apply these fundamental musical elements to appropriate musical situations without being able to consciously think about harmonic functions (tonic, dominant, pre-dominant chords) or scale-step functions (tonic, supertonic, mediant... or I, II, III...). For instance, tonic pedals or framing progressions would appear at the beginning of pieces or sections, not amid mobile progressions (where bass scales, sequences, and the like, were appropriate). Likewise, cadential progressions (what we call root-position dominant-to-tonic progressions) occur at endings of sections or pieces (with the dominant often elaborated by one of a number of standard dominant-pedal progressions), and may also appear right before the appearance of a significant chord (like the dividing dominant in the bass scale in the C-major Prelude). Lastly, more mobile progressions would neither begin nor end phrases.

GIOVANNI PAOLO COLONNA AND PETRONIO FRANCESCHINI:
BUILDING ACOUSTICS AND COMPOSITIONAL STYLE IN LATE SEVENTEENTH-CENTURY BOLOGNA*

Marc Vanscheeuwijck

Traditionally, the "Bologna school" has been associated primarily with trumpet concertos by Giuseppe Torelli or Domenico Gabrielli, or more recently with its hallmark large-scale vocal-instrumental compositions for eight or nine soloists, double choir, trumpets, strings and basso continuo. Although the instrumental compositions represent only about 12% of the total musical output for San Petronio during the last thirty years of the seventeenth century, the large-scale compositions in *stile concertato* are a little more representative of the real San Petronio repertoire (almost 60% of the total output). We also should not forget the numerous smaller-scale compositions — usually for one to four solo voices — with or without *ripieno* choir and the more traditional double-choir repertoire in *stile antico* (almost 30% of the total output).[1]

In this article, I will focus exclusively on the large-scale concerted compositions, which some composers often set in extremely dense counterpoint. In a building as vast as the Bolognese San Petronio Basilica, which has a reverberation time of approximately twelve seconds as well as other peculiar acoustic phenomena, the use of dense counterpoint might seem absurd, and this alleged impracticality has been the cause of much speculation and many questions regarding performance practice. In my work on the late seventeenth-century repertoire in San Petronio, I came across some

---

* An earlier, shorter version of this work was presented at the Tenth Annual Conference of the Society for Seventeenth-Century Music at Princeton University in April 2002.
1. Marc Vanscheeuwijck, "The City and the Church. Music, Liturgy, and Government in late seventeenth-Century Bologna", in: Bruno Bouckaert and Eugeen Schreurs (eds.), *Musical Life in Collegiate Churches in the Low Countries and Europe*, Leuven, 2000, pp. 261–262.

striking stylistic differences not only in the music of the various personalities who wrote for the church, but also as a consequence of the specific position or rank of these musicians within the *Cappella Musicale*. After a short review of the history of the basilica and its context, I will discuss some of the most salient acoustic phenomena and their generic repercussions on the music. In the final section I will compare a representative composition by Giovanni Paolo Colonna (*Maestro di Cappella* from 1674 to 1695) to one by Petronio Franceschini (cellist in San Petronio from 1666 to his death in 1680) and show how these musicians dealt in very different ways with the acoustics of the building. I will argue that because of his function as *Maestro di Cappella*—and also as an important representative member of the Accademia Filarmonica —Colonna was always under pressure to compose in a "higher", more learned (i.e., contrapuntal) style than subordinate composers. Franceschini on the other hand was probably more free to write in a simpler style, the effect of which was acoustically successful also beyond the *Cappella Maggiore* (choir area) of the basilica where only the musical, ecclesiastical, and civic authorities were attending the service. Because of its simplicity Franceschini's music remains intelligible anywhere in the building, while Colonna's has optimal effects only in the semi-enclosed choir. Such an assertion can unfortunately only be completely validated through a listening experience of that music in the church itself. Even recordings —several of which were made by the Cappella Musicale di San Petronio, conducted by Sergio Vartolo, between 1986 and 1991[2]— distort the effect the music has on the listener when present in the basilica.

* * *

With the discovery in 1141 of the remains of Petronius—Bologna's fifth-century bishop—in Santo Stefano, a real cult developed around the saint, who was promptly elevated to patron and protector of the city. However, it took the Bolognese Senate nearly two and a half centuries to decide upon the construction of a large

---

2. Recorded on the label Tactus (TC650001, TC630390).

church dedicated to San Petronio. In 1390 architect Antonio di Vincenzo was charged with drawing up plans for the new church. Unusually for most churches (but typical for its civic function), the Gothic church was built on a north-south orientation with its façade on the Piazza Maggiore (to the north) next to other civic *palazzi*. Although building campaigns went on until 1674, the church was never finished. Only the nave with six arcades was built; the sixth of these became the large choir, when a semi-circular apse was added to it. Indeed, even the façade remains unfinished.[3]

On 4 October 1436 a musical chapel was officially installed by pope Eugene IV, and only six days later a list of twenty-four paid clerics had already been compiled. Cardinal Angelo Capranica elevated the basilica to collegiate church in 1464. Seven years later, in 1471, the vestry board or *Fabbriceria* decided to finance the construction of a 24-foot organ with ten independent stops by the Tuscan builder Lorenzo di Giacomo from Prato. Finished in 1475 and restored by Giovanni Battista Facchetti from Brescia in 1531, the instrument is still intact, and is now located *in cornu epistolae*, and a second instrument built by Baldassarre Malamini in 1596, is now on *in cornu evangeliae* (the Gospel-side). From 1657 on — when Maurizio Cazzati reformed the *Cappella*—the number of regularly paid musicians varied between twenty-eight and thirty-four, including at least twelve singers (not counting the two boys' choirs), two organists, three violinists, two alto violists, one tenor viola player, two *violone* players, one theorbo player, and one sackbut player.[4] Only for special occasions, such as the annual celebration of the San Petronio feast on 4 October, were additional musicians hired. Some of the most spectacular services in the late seventeenth century employed up to 120 musicians.

---

3. Marc Vanscheeuwijck, *The Cappella Musicale of San Petronio in Bologna under Giovanni Paolo Colonna (1674–95)*, Brussels and Rome 2003, pp. 45–54. For more details about the building history, ibid. pp. 47–59, and Cassa di Risparmio di Bologna (ed.), *La Basilica di San Petronio*, 2 vols., Milan 1983–84.
4. ibid., pp. 79–80. Bologna, Archivio della Fabbriceria di San Petronio, *Mandati di pagamento*, cart. 602 (1630–1669), December 1658.

At this point, I should discuss a few general principles of acoustics and their application to the specific case of San Petronio, relying on two fundamental types of sources: the human ear and my own experience of six years as a baroque cellist in the "renewed" *Cappella Musicale* (1986–1992). Although I recognize the unscientific nature of this approach, I contend that a personal, physical experience of the "behavior" of sounds and harmonies in the building itself, using compositions meant to be performed in it, is often more reliable than acoustic theories and oscilloscopes, statistics and abstract calculations, which in some cases end up differing from aural perception. Even though one may indeed hear what one wants or expects to hear, I tried to limit such subjective impressions by asking several listeners and musicians who participated in the recording projects mentioned above for their perceptions. Composers and musicians of the seventeenth century trusted their ears and experience when writing their music and in determining the optimal instrumentation for it. Although I was not able to find many of their observations about specific acoustical problems in the basilica in any of my primary sources, a few general comments are sufficiently symptomatic of the particular acoustics of the church. In his booklet with guidelines for the *Maestro di Cappella* and his collaborators published in 1658, Maurizio Cazzati admonishes the musicians not to leave the choir before the director allows them to, because the noise could disturb the reverberation:

> *Non dovrà alcuno abbandonare la Cappella sotto qual si voglia pretesto senza licenza del Mastro, il quale nel concederla habbi riguardo di lasciar la musica piena in modo, che porti il solito rimbombo alla Chiesa sino al fine del servitio cominciato.*[5]

In the polemic between Cazzati's successor Giovanni Paolo Colonna and Arcangelo Corelli about the famous parallel fifths in mm. 3-6 of the *Allemande* of the latter's Sonata Opus II/3, which yielded an epistolary exchange between the two protagon-

---

5. Maurizio Cazzati (?), *ORDINI Per la Musica dell'Insigne Collegiata di S. Petronio, Reformati d'ordine de gl'Illustrissimi Signori Presidente, e Fabbricieri della Reverenda Fabbrica di essa*, Bologna 1658, p. 5.

ists and others such as Matteo Zani and Antimo Liberati from 26 September to 12 December 1685, Colonna mentions—again *en passant*—that certain "liberties" in counterpoint may be visible in the score, but often do not disturb the ear because they may be meant for a special effect, particularly in a space such as S. Petronio where large numbers of musicians are involved in polychoral music:

> *Nella mia capella di S.Petronio per la festa del Santo, che con gran decoro, e nobiltà si soleniza faccio cantare molte mie compositioni à tre, e [fol. 40v] quatro chori, et hò questo singolare honore ogn'anno, che compariscono bravi virtuosi, et eccellenti M[aest]ri di Capella, sì di Lombardia, come di Venezia, et altri luoghi p[er] sentire q[uel]la funtione riguardevoliss[i]ma sì per la qualità de Musici virtuosi, come p[er] la quantità assendendo al numero di 130 incirca, quando più, quando meno, secondo che commandano i Patroni; hora questi eccellenti virtuosi alle volte hanno fatto gran caso di molti passi tanto di concerto grosso, quanto di concertino picciolo, che se gli havessero havuti sotto gl'oc[c]hi haverebbero trovato qualche eccett[io]ne p[er] qualche licenza, la quale sarà stata il condimento di quel passo, che tanto hanno stimato, e se si fosse levata questa licenza, et autenticato questo passo, al certo non haverebbe cavato quest'effetto, che gli apportò [fol. 41r] tanta sodisfattione; mà parlo sempre di quelle licenze che apportano buoni effetti, avvertendo che siano bene assicurati le parti superiori, e le mancanze, e passi pericolosi per diminuzione, e per qualche altra mancanza darla alle parti inferiori che dagl'istessi professori non saranno mai conosciute, ne considerate;[…].*[6]

Colonna's comment refers even less directly than Cazzati's to the acoustics of the church, but at least it acknowledges the fact that the sound result in San Petronio can "mask" certain contrapuntal liberties.

The acoustic of San Petronio has often been described as problematic, difficult or defective, but I have tried to approach it more positively: the particular sound characteristics of the building guided and stimulated composers to adapt their compositional style to achieve the best sound result possible. For my purposes in this

---

6. Bologna, Civico Museo Bibliografico Musicale, ms. D. 1, n° 7: *Risposta del Sr. Gio: Paolo Colonna alla Replica fatta dal Sr. Liberati*, 12 December 1685, fol. 40r-41r.

study, the discipline of acoustics was actually not as helpful as I had hoped it would be. Aside from purely theoretical, usually mathematical approaches, the literature on the subject of acoustic results in Gothic churches is limited, and an orientation toward musical or compositional choices and/or limitations based on acoustical phenomena is almost completely foreign to the discipline.[7]

In San Petronio two fundamental acoustical phenomena strike even the most absent-minded visitor: first, the unusually long reverberation time and second, the spontaneous enhancement of the (pure) major third as a result (during the reverberation) of the buildup of the resonance of a low pitch (or its octave) and its fifth.[8] Since both these phenomena can be heard clearly by playing just one chord on one of the organs, I will consider them first. Additional phenomena will be discussed subsequently.

Reverberation time is the time needed for the energy of a sound wave—after the sound signal has ceased to be emitted—to be reduced to a millionth (-60dB) of its original energy. The para-

---

7. Dorothea Baumann, "Musical Acoustics in the Middle Ages", in: *Early Music* 18 (1990), pp. 199–210, and Katelijne Schiltz, "Church and Chamber: the Influence of Acoustics on Musical Composition and Performance", in: *Early Music* 31 (2003), pp. 64–78 are recent exceptions. Although acoustics as a discipline began to develop in the Baroque era, none of the scientists ventured into problems of room acoustics: see Sigalia Dostrovsky and John T. Cannon, "Entstehung der musikalischen Akustik (1600–1750)", in: Frieder Zaminer (ed.), *Geschichte der Musiktheorie, Band. 6: Hören, messen und rechnen in der frühen Neuzeit*, Darmstadt 1987, pp. 7–79.

8. This phenomenon can possibly be explained by the fact that in a space as large as San Petronio, in which the "room dimensions are larger than the wavelength of the lowest frequency, 30 ft [9.144 m] or more, the [normal vibration] modes are closely spaced in frequency and the room will react reasonably uniformly to broad band sound at low frequencies" (H. J. Purkis, *Building Physics: Acoustics*, London 1966, p. 95). In other words, when sufficiently low frequencies (roughly between 25Hz and 100Hz) are played on the organs (in the 24 and/or 16-foot range), the fourth overtone or fifth harmonic (i.e. the major third in the third octave above the fundamental, or the upper seventeenth) will be audible if enough time is given to allow for a buildup of the resonance in the space. Since such low pitches are consistently used in large-scale *concertato* music for solemn celebrations in San Petronio, and the long reverberation time of the basilica permits such a gradual buildup of resonance, the listener will clearly perceive the major third after a few seconds of reverberation. (I wish to thank Prof. Michael Raymer of the Department of Physics at the University of Oregon for clarifying this for me, and Prof. Dr. Rudolf Rasch who suggested that I revisit this issue).

meters influencing this loss of energy are the volume of the space, the total surface of walls and objects that can reflect sound waves, and the average absorption coefficient of the materials present in the room. For the particular case of San Petronio, we know only the volume of the building (12,408,048 cubic feet or 351.148m³) and the average reverberation time, which is approximately twelve seconds. This may vary, depending on the intensity, tempo, and frequency of the sound signal, and on the noise inside the church. Twelve seconds is the maximal figure I measured during evening rehearsals (the church was locked, there were no visitors, and noise from traffic was reduced) after a final major triad performed by a large mixed vocal and instrumental ensemble. During the day, surrounding noises (visitors, cleaning crews, city buses, cars, and motorcycles) reduce the audible reverberation time to approximately ten seconds. Whether acoustics with such a long reverberation time can be classified as "good" is solely an aesthetic question, which depends partly on the expectation patterns of a listener, and partly on the specific function of the space under consideration.

The twelve-second reverberation time in the church notwithstanding, the acoustics within the *Cappella Maggiore* behind the altar actually allow for exceptional clarity of the music. Whoever is located in the choir (which contains one hundred and forty-five choir stalls, where the clergy and the civic authorities were seated) finds himself in the middle between the two organs, and singers and instrumentalists projected their sound from above on the semi-circular platform behind the horseshoe-shaped balustrades (*quando si faceva Cappella*).[9] This way the civic authorities, the clergy, the members of the Accademia Filarmonica, and the representatives of the university received a combination of directly projected sound waves and their reflection against the vault and

---

9. The only acoustic problem is actually one for the musicians themselves, not for the listeners in the choir: with the two organs (and their respective continuo groups and choirs) being almost twenty meters (sixty-five feet) apart from each other, and from the third group with the trumpets, upper strings, and the orchestra continuo instruments, each of these ensembles hears the others with a sufficiently disturbing delay. Given that sound travels at a speed of 344 m/s, the direct waves should theoretically reach the musicians in 0.172 s; but in reality the reflected waves predominate over the direct waves in the musicians' perception, causing a longer *perceived* delay.

against the wooden choir walls, the highly ornamental features, reliefs, niches, columns, and sculptures which had the same absorbing function as the *frons scenae* of an ancient Roman theatre (as in Orange). In the nave, and even in the aisles behind the choir walls, this absorbing effect of the wooden organ cases and of the *ajouré* panels is no longer audible, and the sound waves that reach listeners' ears there are only reflected waves. Consequently, for twelve seconds a chord will keep mixing itself—though with strongly decreasing intensity—with all subsequently emitted sounds, which may enhance the fullness of that chord in a sometimes impressive manner.

For important holidays, moreover, the church was usually adorned. In addition to the payments for musicians for the San Petronio celebrations, there are usually receipts, for example (in 1679) to Giacomo Bovi *addobbatore* ("who adorns the church"), who was paid for buying the yellow and red cloth and for hanging it in the basilica.[10] From the *"Insignia" degli Anziani* in the Archivio di Stato (i.e., the commemorative images of the most significant events during the two-month mandates of the *Gonfaloniere* and the *Anziani*) we know that these draperies in the colors of the city adorned the balustrades and the columns. Sometimes they were also hung as curtains in the top of the vaults between the bays and between nave and aisles. (See Ill. 1) How much these draperies actually reduced the reverberation time is hard to estimate. During the concerts for the feast day of San Petronio in 1986–1991 such draperies were used to adorn the choir (not the columns nor the vaults), but they had no audible effect:

---

10. Archivio della Fabbriceria di San Petronio, *Liste e Ricevute (Filze di Cassa)*, cart. 578 (1678–1684), n° 553: *Nota delle Spese p[er] la Festa del Glorioso S. Petronio in/ Musici, Addobbo, Messe, et altre spese come segue e pma./*: "A Ms Giacomo Adobatore p[er] spese minute p[er] Adobbo come/ da nota n° 5 £14.6/ Al med[esim]o p[er] fitto di Veli, Cendaline, et adobbi ~~come n[ot]a n° 6~~ £74. The document offers more details in Nota 6:

Veli Gialli Pezze/ n° 100	£50
Cendaline n° 20	£12
Adobbi Rossi e Gialli	£12
	£74"

Building Acoustics and Compositional Style

the acoustics in the choir remained as full and direct as before, nor was the reverberation time reduced in the remainder of the church. Even when the church was filled with people — i.e., with six thousand to nine thousand people present — I still measured a reverberation time of nine and a half seconds.

Another phenomenon is that in the reverberation of a major triad the last pitch to decay is always the major third, which appears as the loudest sound in the chord. Already after the third second, this third begins to dominate. Experiments with open fifth chords played in the lowest two octaves of the organs provided the astonishing effect that a non-generated major third (as a fundamental frequency) occurred anyway, and could be clearly heard, though never too predominantly. It is thus sufficient to play a (low) pitch, its upper fifth and its octave on one of the organs to hear the major third as well (see footnote 8). An ideal result is obtained when, for example, in a mixed vocal and instrumental composition with eighteen parts, only two or at most three inner parts (tenors or altos) sing or play the major third. The eventual balance between tonics, fifths, and thirds will be perfect and maintained as such until the total decay of the sound. On the other hand, in a final minor triad, the generated minor third starts to enter in dissonance with the major third induced by the acoustics. In Bolognese music, needless to say, we never find a minor third in a strong final chord.

The remaining acoustical phenomena are related to this long reverberation time and the effect of resonance. In general, low frequencies are the first to be absorbed, because they easily enter into resonance with the proper frequencies of the materials of the wall surfaces (which are low), causing the sound waves to be deprived of their energy.[11] To counteract this the old organ was given a

---

11. The absorption coefficient of hard surfaces (stone floor, walls and vaults in plastered brick, wooden surfaces) is typically higher for low than for high frequencies. On the other hand wooden chairs, the presence of people in the church, and the cloth used for occasional adornment tend to absorb the higher frequencies more. However, in a space as large as San Petronio these factors have a relatively small influence. In large rooms we also need to include air absorption, but here again, the typically high humidity level of the air in Bologna becomes relevant only at frequencies so high

24-foot stop (i.e., a 32' starting from ²F), and in the vocal and instrumental ensembles performing in the basilica the basses (and double basses) were heavily reinforced in number (to almost 45% of the total ensemble), compared to the higher-pitched instruments. It also needs to be recalled that none of the bass instruments (including cellos, *violoni*, double basses, theorboes, and the organs with their low wind pressure) could compete with the intensity of the sound of violins and trumpets. On the other hand the power and intensity of a solo bass voice or of a (*castrato*) soprano could better suit the acoustics of the building than a solo tenor or alto voice, which was almost immediately absorbed. High frequencies are sensitive to absorption by the clothing of musicians, clergy and congregation, whereas for the bright trumpet sounds — partly also given their intensity — a long reverberation time can be extremely flattering.

These observations yield a few provisional conclusions, which I will show in the musical examples. Although the basilica of San Petronio has an acoustic which can be characterized first and foremost by an unusually long reverberation time, it induces no damaging effects such as echo or exaggerated sound mixing. When sound waves cease to be emitted, a small shock wave occurs, followed by a maximum twelve-second smooth decay. However, this is true only for the nave of the church, in which the congregation could only be overwhelmed by the fullness and the plasticity of the sounds. The privileged classes in the choir were able to enjoy clearly articulated sounds since the sound waves literally flowed over them from above (the distant reverberation in the nave is heard in the choir, but its intensity is quite low). The main acoustic difference between the nave and the *Cappella Maggiore*

(above 8000Hz) that they virtually never occur in the repertoire under consideration. The reverberation time (T) for large auditoria and rooms is expressed in the equation $T = 0.161 \times V/Sa + mV$, in which 0.161 is a constant value, V is the total volume of the space (in m³), S is the total surface (in m2), a is the average absorption coefficient, and m is the absorption coefficient of the air (in m-1). See Thomas D. Rossing, *The Science of Sound*, Reading Massachusetts 1982, pp. 430–432; John Backus, *The Acoustical Foundations of Music*, New York 1969, pp. 143–159; and Harvey and Donald White, *Physics and Music*, Philadelphia 1980, pp. 365–369.

(i.e. the choir) is that in the choir direct sound waves dominate over reflected waves (reverberation), whereas elsewhere in the church the reverse is true. The perception of the presence of the pure major third is a constant factor, while the absorption of low string sounds and of quiet soprano voices is the only phenomenon which the presence of a large number of listeners will affect in an audible way.

In this final section, I will take a brief look at two musical examples, a *Dixit Dominus* by Colonna (datable in the late 1670s) and a *Dixit Dominus* of 1676 by Petronio Franceschini, to explore how both composers, very aware of the limitations imposed by the acoustics, seemed to have written their music for different "parts" of the congregation.

The example I have chosen is Colonna's *Dixit à 9 conc^{to}: con V.V./ è RR/ G.P.C. Parti/ N° 92* (GPC. 183).[12] (See Ex. 1) In traditional San Petronio style, the *Dixit Dominus* opens on two large chords on the tonic and dominant of E minor, followed by a homorhythmic declamation of the first half verse by choir 1, while choir 2 elaborates along with the instruments on the second half of the first verse in what I would call pseudopolyphony. In this entire tutti section the harmony remains on the tonic of E minor, with chords mostly in root position. The solo section in a faster tempo is set in simple imitative counterpoint in which two types of melodies are presented: a motif on repeated pitches in eighth-note values, with a leap of a fourth or fifth, respectively (*Donec ponam inimicos*), contrasted by a short motif of four quarter notes with an upbeat (on *scabellum pedum*). Further on, in the tutti section, these two "themes" are combined in a pseudo double fugue, after which the *scabellum pedum* motif is developed with typically instrumental figures. The harmonization of this short

---

12. The manuscript score is preserved in the Österreichische Nationalbibliothek in Vienna, Cod. 15518. The ninety-two original parts (now lost) represent a fairly average but nonetheless quite large number of performers for a composition intended for the celebration of San Petronio (on 4 October) and included instrumental parts for first and second violins, alto and tenor violas, basses (cellos, *violoni*, and double basses); nine vocal soloists (SSATB in choir 1, and SATB in choir 2), and as many *ripieno* parts; and a general basso continuo.

Building Acoustics and Compositional Style

postlude remains in E minor and closes on a chord with a Picardy third (in the alto viola part). The more frequent occurrence of suspensions and anticipations introduced in the solo section, by virtue of which the composer briefly creates seventh and ninth chords, is only maintained in the closing tutti section in passages in *contrappunto legato* (on *inimicos*). I have mentioned earlier how the major third is clearly perceived as an overtone of a low pitch and its fifth in San Petronio. Both the fact that Colonna always utilized a Picardy third in loud final chords in music written for San Petronio, and that as much as possible he tried to keep this major third "hidden" in the texture (in order to avoid the major third still becoming audible after a reverberation time of nine or ten seconds), constitute, I believe, convincing proof that the composer consciously had this acoustic phenomenon in mind when he conceived his music for the Basilica. The overall sound effect of this section is fairly complex even though the counterpoint remains reasonably simple, although we need to keep in mind that the listeners located in the choir probably included the only musically educated personalities. This movement actually sounds like a large unintelligible sea of sound elsewhere in the church, the enormity of which could only have overwhelmed the average member of the congregation. In the second movement (on verse 3 of the psalm: *Virgam virtutis tuae emittet Dominus ex Sion*) Colonna set the text for four solo voices (SATB) with basso continuo, using imitative counterpoint in a late seventeenth-century version of *stile antico*. Although the section appears to be in B minor, it shows clear affinities with the Hypodorian mode transposed *in epidiapente* (to E, with one # in the key signature, and the *initialis* and *finalis* on B).[13] The composer keeps playing with G (even on the seventh degree) and G# throughout this section, thus maintaining tonal ambiguity between E major and E minor. In the cadence at the conclusion of this Allegro section in triple meter, Colonna avoids the third in the chord, but in the last four meas-

---

13. According to Bononcini a piece in the Hypodorian mode, beginning on the normal *initialis* on the fifth degree (B), can exceptionally also end on the same degree (Giovanni Maria Bononcini, *Musico Prattico*, Bologna 1673, p. 154).

ures of the movement (Adagio; pure homophony; duple meter), he obviously moves to the key of B minor with a Picardy third in the tenor voice. Whereas this entire "modal" movement serves as a contrast to the preceding and following movements, which are tonally much more stable, the third movement, a *Devisenarie* (motto aria) for soprano and bass solo, strings and continuo on the fourth verse of the psalm (*Tecum principium*) is clearly written in G major with only a couple of passages in the dominant key. The entire section is again highly effective for the acoustics of the church: a clearly delineated walking bass serves as a background to the melodious soprano and bass solos (in dialogue), which are only occasionally interrupted by short homophonic commentaries of the strings, which conclude the movement with the usual short (eight-measure) postlude. In the next movement, Colonna returns to his colossal style in which he seeks powerful contrasts in tempo, performing forces, and texture. He finally builds up a huge climax to conclude the section in complex counterpoint on *confregit reges* in E minor with a Picardy third only in the second violins and second sopranos of the first choir. I cannot describe each of the sections in full here, but in the conclusive movement of the psalm on the doxology, Colonna opens in a short and swift passage in free counterpoint and proceeds (on *Sicut erat in principio*) into an impressive section in fugal counterpoint. Typically, the composer does not develop his fugue beyond the entrance of the nine vocal parts (*soli* and *ripieni*) and five instrumental parts, moving into a homophonic cadential section (on *et nunc et semper*), which yields a new fugal buildup in faster tempo on *et in saecula saeculorum*, to conclude homophonically again on *Amen* in E minor with a Picardy third in the first violins, the altos of choir I, and the tenors of choir II.

It is striking that Colonna so rarely uses altos or tenors as soloists in his large-scale compositions (except in combination with all the other soloists in ensemble movements), whether in this *Dixit Dominus*, or in his other works. On the other hand he never hesitates to write spectacular solos for sopranos or basses. Although Colonna often writes in imitative counterpoint, he limits such textures to sections in which he uses the vocal soloists and basso continuo only. However, when he utilizes larger forces, including *ripieni* and instruments, he always begins in imitative counterpoint, but quickly moves into homophonic textures, keeping the overwhelming and most complex textures for the final climax in conclusion of a composition in "colossal" style.

A comparison with a typical example of Franceschini's compositional style is extremely revealing. Petronio Franceschini, born in Bologna on 9 January 1651, was regularly hired (between 1666 and 1674) as an extra musician for the San Petronio celebrations. After his teacher Giovanni Battista Vitali departed for Modena, and shortly after Colonna was elected in November 1674 to *Maestro di Cappella*, Franceschini was appointed cellist in the *Cappella* on 6 March 1675, a post he held until his death in Venice on 4 December 1680. His role in composing sacred music for the liturgy in San Petronio was quite important. With a large repertoire of liturgical music, including several masses and psalms with one or two trumpets, Franceschini was (among the instrumentalists of the *Cappella*) undoubtedly the most prolific composer in the twenty-one years of Colonna's tenure as *Maestro*.[14] Franceschini's *Dixit Dominus A 8, con stromenti*,[15] composed for the San Petronio celebration 1676, is very representative of his large-scale compositions for voices and instruments. (See Ex. 2)

Franceschini's double-choir compositions, all dated between 1674 and 1680, feature a number of remarkable technical characteristics. In general, and in opposition to Colonna, he consistently avoids complex textures in imitative *contrappunto legato*, including in the final tutti sections of his masses, canticles and psalms. Choir settings are mainly homorhythmic; like Colonna, when Franceschini has the various parts begin fugally, he usually lets them merge into a strictly chordal texture as soon as the last imitating part has exposed its thematic material. The difference from

---

14. Vanscheeuwijck, *The Cappella Musicale of San Petronio in Bologna under Giovanni Paolo Colonna (1674–95)*, Brussels and Rome 2003, pp. 155–56.
15. The manuscript is preserved in Bologna, Archivio Musicale di San Petronio (Lib. F.III.2) and is scored for trumpet in D, first and second violins, alto and tenor violas, basses; eight vocal soloists (SATB in choir 1 and SATB in choir 2) and as many *ripieni* parts; and a general basso continuo.

Building Acoustics and Compositional Style

Building Acoustics and Compositional Style

Building Acoustics and Compositional Style

Building Acoustics and Compositional Style

Building Acoustics and Compositional Style

Colonna however, is that Franceschini never juxtaposes several such passages within one section, and he always keeps them extremely short. Imitative counterpoint generally appears only in solo passages, whereas the composer suggests imitation through the fast alternation of short rhythmic and melodic formulas performed by various contrasting voice and instrument combinations (including soloists and larger ensembles). His melodies typically consist of short cells mostly elaborated rhythmically. The opening of his 1676 *Dixit Dominus* is a typical case in point: after two long D major chords including strings, the two choirs, and continuo (on *Dixit*), the trumpet repeats the two D pitches with continuo alone, after which the other forces come back with a homophonic iteration of *Dixit Dominus* (in note values twice as fast), followed by its exact imitation by the trumpet and continuo. Again, the large forces come back to build up more of the text (*Dixit Dominus Domino meo*), in again twice-as-fast dactylic rhythms, followed by the imitation of the trumpet. These last two measures are then repeated before the trumpet plays a short postlude introducing the two measures sung in unison by the altos of both choirs (with continuo) on *Sede a dextris meis*. The composer repeats this entire sequence of events in the dominant key, having thus presented all the musical ingredients he will use throughout this opening fifty-nine-measure movement.

Compared to Colonna, Franceschini limits himself to one or two short and simple rhythmic motifs which penetrate quite clearly through the reverberant acoustics of the basilica. His harmonic rhythm is even slower than Colonna's and the keys are mostly limited to tonic and dominant, even in the sections where the trumpet does not play. In the second movement (on the second verset *Donec ponam inimicos tuos*) Franceschini also uses reduced forces: altos, tenors, and basses of the first choir (probably used soloistically, though no indication of this is mentioned in the score) with basso continuo. Melodies are again short cells in which the composer opposes a short ascending motif in slower rhythm to a faster descending motif (on *inimicos*), refraining from introducing more than these two basic ingredients. Moreover, he maintains the same ideas in the following tutti section without trumpet (on *Virgam virtutis*), but instead of a fast descending motif he uses repeated pitches (on *dominare*). Again, I will not describe the entire composition, but I should mention that Franceschini uses more solo sections than Colonna: movement three, *Tecum principium*, is for alto solo (a rarity also in Franceschini's music) with two solo violins; *Juravit Dominus* is set for soprano solo and trumpet solo, to be contrasted by a fairly homophonic SATB-and-continuo setting of the *Dominus a dextris tuis*. In the closing movement on the doxology, Franceschini mainly opposes the tutti with solos of the joint soprano or alto parts, and the dactylic rhythmic cells of the opening movement are still his most noticeable compositional ingredient. The *Amen*, in triple meter has two- or three-measure imitative entrances in voices and instruments, but as opposed to Colonna, Franceschini plays more with antiphonal contrasts between the separate choirs and the instruments, to conclude in a mainly homophonic colossal tutti. The stylistic features I describe here are by no means unique to this composition, they are quite representative of Franceschini's style in general.

It seems to me that Franceschini even more than Colonna was conscious of working with the acoustics of San Petronio in his compositions. Colonna dared to write sometimes poignant but highly expressive dissonances or complex *contrappunto legato*, knowing that this could be heard and valued in the choir but not elsewhere in the basilica. Franceschini on the other hand consistently wrote in a rhythmically very articulated homophonic style with few dissonances, broad harmonic planes, virtually no modulations, and highly contrasting alternations of vocal and instrumental colors. As *Maestro di Cappella*, Colonna composed for the civic and ecclesiastic authorities who were placed in the choir behind the altar. Although both composers obviously tried to maximize the quality of the overall sound result of their music by adapting it to the acoustic characteristics of the church, Franceschini was perhaps more interested in what the congregation on the other side of the altar was able to hear; in that sense he may be considered a more populist composer than the rather elitist Colonna. He seems to have fully accepted the acoustic characteristics of the building, knowing exactly what sort of effects he could obtain and provoke in it, without trying to overcome them, as Colonna did, or maybe had to do.

Obviously, Franceschini's music is extremely well adapted — but also *only* adapted — to the acoustics of San Petronio, meaning that the performance of most of his compositions in other, less reverberant acoustical environments would make his music appear to be uninspired or even simplistic. Although Franceschini was certainly not discouraged from publishing any of his works, he was by no means under any pressure to do so. After all, his only obligation towards the *Cappella* was to appear for all the services in which he was needed as a cellist. Nowhere in the archival documents extant in San Petronio have I found any mention of Franceschini's duties as an assistant composer to the *Maestro*, nor have I encountered any trace of remuneration for his efforts. Colonna, on the other hand, being the *Maestro di Cappella* of one of the most important churches in the Papal States and of the city church of Bologna (considered more important to the city authorities than the Cathedral of San Pietro) was a much more important public figure, whose work as a composer continued to be scrutinized by colleagues and authorities alike. Although he did not publish much before his appointment as *Maestro* in the basilica in 1674 (at the age of 37!), he eventually caught up, having four collections of sacred works printed in 1681–82, which contained almost fifty compositions. Throughout his career he continued to publish more sacred music (twelve collections containing 114 pieces in total), of which only Opus X and XII consist of large-scale concerted music in a style comparable to the approximately 100 compositions extant in manuscript only, in the Österreichische Nationalbibliothek in Vienna. It is clear that, through his publication efforts, Colonna thus intended at least some of his works to be performed elsewhere, which would also partly explain his tendency to not fully adapt his compositional style to the acoustics of the San Petronio basilica as Franceschini did.

In sum, through the works of Franceschini, who clearly wrote music to be performed in San Petronio, it is possible to identify a number of musical ingredients that needed to be adapted to the particular acoustics of the building in order to maximize the sound effect in the church. Given his leading position not only in the basilica, but also as a composer of some renown in various Italian cities, Colonna was forced to compromise more than his colleague, so that his compositions could withstand scrutiny in a broader musical world. His decision to publish and disseminate a number of his compositions naturally also constrained him to produce a repertoire that corresponded more to the mainstream styles of sacred music in the late seventeenth century. In the compositions he did not revise for publication, however, his style remains more idiomatic to a typical "San Petronio style", due in the first place to the acoustic characteristics the building offers.

Finally, I believe it to be fundamentally important for the twenty-first-century scholar and performer alike to consider acoustic matters in both the analysis of certain compositions and in programming them for public performances. In reading invariably positive contemporary accounts of the quality of the music produced for San Petronio in the period 1670–1700, I was not able to reconcile them with what I saw in the scores. It is only through a consideration of acoustic characteristics in the church that I could begin to understand why such able contrapuntists wrote the way they did. In the same vein, it would make little sense to attempt a performance of this music in a modern, non-reverberant concert hall. Although the acoustics of San Petronio represent a fairly exceptional situation, we need to keep in mind that the Bolognese basilica was by no means the only very large reverberant church in the Catholic world, and that extant sacred compositions which were never revised for publication might benefit from a reconsideration (by analysts and performers) that includes knowledge about acoustic matters and questions about how composers dealt with them.

PERSONALIA

Personalia

THOMAS CHRISTENSEN

Thomas Christensen took his Ph.D. at Yale in 1985, and is Professor of Music at the University of Chicago since 1999. He is a theorist and historian of music theory with special interests in eighteenth-century intellectual history, problems in tonal theory, historiography, and aesthetics. He is the author of numerous books and articles, including *Rameau and Musical Thought in the Enlightenment* (Cambridge 1993). Most recently (2002) he has edited the *Cambridge History of Western Music Theory*. He served as President of the Society for Music Theory (1999–2001), and is the recipient of numerous awards and fellowships.

PENELOPE GOUK

Penelope Gouk took her Ph.D. in Combined Studies (History and Music) at the Warburg Institute, University of London in 1982. Until 1994 she held a series of postdoctoral fellowships at Oxford, before moving to the University of Manchester, where she is now a Senior Lecturer in History. She is currently investigating how changes in musical practice fundamentally transformed medical understandings of the human body and psyche between the fifteenth and eighteenth centuries. Her latest books are *Music, Science and Natural Magic in Seventeenth-Century England* (New Haven and London 1999), and, as editor, *Musical Healing in Cultural Contexts* (Aldershot 2000) and *Representing Emotions: New Connections in the Histories of Art, Music and Medicine* (Aldershot 2005).

GERARD GEAY

Gérard Geay studied at the CNSM in Paris, where he obtained first prizes for harmony, counterpoint, fugue, musicology, analysis, and composition. His career as a professor started in 1969 and led him to various conservatories and universities. Between 1974 and 1987, he was a producer at Radio France. In 1986, he devised a curriculum for the department of early music at the conservatory of Lyon, introducing various disciplines like counterpoint, harmony, instrumentation, basso continuo and analysis. He is currently professor of harmony and counterpoint at the departments of early music and of composition. Between 1993 and 1997, he lectured at the Centre de Musique Médiévale in Paris. He is a regular collaborator to the Centre de Musique Baroque at Versailles, where he supervises the *Cahiers de Musique* collection and is one of the driving forces behind the research project "L'Art de composer en France aux XVIIe et XVIIIe siècles".

SUSAN MCCLARY

Susan McClary took her Ph.D. at Harvard in 1976, taught at the University of Minnesota and McGill University in Montreal, and is now Professor of Musicology at the University of California, Los Angeles. She specializes in the cultural criticism of music, both the European canon and contemporary popular genres. She is author of *Feminine Endings: Music, Gender, and Sexuality* (Minneapolis 1991), *Georges Bizet: Carmen* (Cambridge 1992), and *Conventional Wisdom: The Content of Musical Form* (Berkeley 2000). Her more recent publications explore the many ways in which subjectivities have been construed in music from the sixteenth century onward. She won the 2005 Otto Kinkeldey Prize for *Modal Subjectivities: Renaissance Self-Fashioning in the Italian Madrigal* (Berkeley 2004) and is now working on *Power and Desire in Seventeenth-Century Music*.

MARKUS JANS

Markus Jans studied piano and clarinet at the Lucerne Conservatory, music theory and composition at the Musikhochschule in Basle, and musicology at the University of Basle. Since 1972 he has been teaching "Historische Satzlehre" at the Schola Cantorum Basiliensis and since 1979 History of Music Theory at the Musikhochschule in Basle. Since 1972 he has also been active as a choral conductor. Publications in various different periodicals such as the *Jahrbuch für historische Musikpraxis*, *Musiktheorie* and *Musik & Ästhetik*, on topics of setting technique, aesthetics and analysis in the context of the historic approach in music theory.

JOEL LESTER

Joel Lester took his Ph.D. at Princeton in 1970. He also studied violin with Margaret Pardee and Ivan Galamian. In addition to his career as a violinist (e.g. member of the Da Capo Chamber Players), he was appointed professor at The City College and The Graduate School of the City University of New York. He has been Dean of Mannes College in New York City since 1996. As an author, Joel Lester has published, amongst others: *Compositional Theory in the 18th Century* (Cambridge, Mass. 1992), *Harmony in Tonal Music* (New York 1982), *Analytical Approaches to Atonal Music* (New York 1989), *Between Modes and Keys* (Hillsdale, NY 1989), *The Rhythms of Tonal Music* (Carbondale 1986), and *Bach's Works for Solo Violin: Style, Structure, Performance* (Oxford 1999). Joel Lester was President of the Society for Music Theory from 2003–2005.

MARC VANSCHEEUWIJCK

Marc Vanscheeuwijck is a Belgian native who studied art history, romance languages, and musicology at the University of Ghent, where he received his Ph.D. in 1995. After graduating from the Bruges and Ghent Conservatories in cello and chamber music in 1986, he studied Baroque cello with Wouter Möller, and moved to Bologna, to do research in seventeenth-century Bolognese music. Since 1995, he has been on the music history faculty at the University of Oregon in Eugene, where he also directs the Collegium Musicum. As a music historian he concentrates his efforts on the use of various types of violoni in the Baroque period, and on seventeenth-century sacred music. His book *The Cappella Musicale of San Petronio in Bologna under Giovanni Paolo Colonna (1674–95). History — Organization — Repertoire* was published in 2003 by the Belgian Historical Institute in Rome.

EDITORS
Sylvester Beelaert
Peter Dejans
Kathleen Snyers

AUTHORS
Thomas Christensen
Penelope Gouk
Gérard Geay
Susan McClary
Markus Jans
Joel Lester
Marc Vanscheeuwijck

LAY-OUT
Filiep Tacq, Ghent/Madrid

PRESS
Grafikon, Oostkamp
Bioset, 100gr

ISBN 978 90 5867 587 3
D/2007/1869/7
NUR 663
© 2007 by Leuven University Press /
Universitaire Pers Leuven / Presses Universitaires de Louvain
Minderbroedersstraat 4, B-3000 Leuven (Belgium)

All rights reserved.
Except in those cases expressly determined by law,
no part of this publication may be multiplied,
saved in automated data file or made public in any way whatsoever
without the express prior written consent of the publishers.